THE SUSTAINABLE TURNAROUND

Fix, reset and accelerate your business
to thrive in 12 months

MADIHA MOUCHTAK MBA

R^ethink

First published in Great Britain in 2021
by Rethink Press (www.rethinkpress.com)

© Copyright Madiha Mouchtak

Cover photograph by Mathilde Maria Nai

Contents

Introduction

You are reading this book for a reason – perhaps your company is experiencing difficulties in the aftermath of the COVID-19 pandemic, the global economic crisis, the Fourth Industrial Revolution, the Great Reset or all of the above. Maybe you are a strategic thinker who sees global economic developments coming and wants to be prepared to weather these changes as quickly and painlessly as possible or maybe you want to improve your business and prepare it for growth in a rapidly changing market. This book will support you to positively influence the destiny of your business and move it towards thriving within twelve months.

Over the past twenty years, I have worked on extremely challenging business transformations and company rescue projects. Whether entrepreneur or transformational leader, I know that when you experience a new threatening phenomenon or external force in your business, you need answers fast. You want them now.

The turnaround books that I reached for had promising titles but were too long and too philosophical, focusing on slashing costs but not providing an end-to-end solution for a sustainable turnaround, or showing how to get there. I wanted this book to be different, a book for business owners, leaders and employee representatives that is concise and has an end-to-end approach supported with data and clear steps. It needed to be a leadership- and people-centric book that provides guidance on how to Fix, Reset and Accelerate a business in twelve months and will help you stay focused, balanced and healthy while leading teams though all-pervasive change, or even crisis, and help them move towards a brighter future.

In 2020 I had just finished a two-year turnaround project, successfully moving the business from losses to a double-digit profit and growth. I was still on a high, enjoying the afterglow of getting the business to a good place, enjoying some time off, reflecting on what I could have done better and faster, doing research, studying to stay up to date with trends and thinking about my next big thing when the COVID-19 pandemic hit. I saw how global bodies such as the World Health Organization (WHO) and International

Monetary Fund (IMF) started telling countries what they should be doing. Meanwhile, the World Economic Forum (WEF) was pushing an agenda about the Fourth Industrial Revolution and a Great Reset of the world economy.

Businesses were being locked down, there was a serious shift in policies and approach, people were asked to stay home, borders closed, and travel bans instigated, all leading to extreme uncertainty. Temporary help was offered by local governments to businesses, as well as provided globally by the IMF and the EU to keep the economy floating and prevent a major collapse and social unrest. This help will not be sufficient and will not last forever. Companies face collapsing demand, decreasing revenues and decreasing exports; layoffs are on the rise, and an economic crisis and recession is boiling up at the magnitude of the Great Depression of the 1930s.

Medium-sized businesses of between 50 and 250 employees, which employ half of the working population in most European countries, were (and will be) the most affected and most at risk.[1] These businesses can't afford expensive consulting services and can't take on big corporates in the demands of the Fourth Industrial Revolution.

---

1 'How many people work in small enterprises?', Eurostat, no date, https://ec.europa.eu/eurostat/web/products-eurostat-news/-/WDN-20180627-1

So the time was now. If I wanted to help to rescue as many companies as possible, I needed to write this book and focus it on the precise steps that companies facing all-pervasive change and crisis need to take.

Overview of the book

In Chapter 1 I will explain what is happening in the world and how you should deal with it. How what is happening could lead to a crisis in your business, what that means and how to solve it will follow in Chapter 2.

As you will be dealing with your own worries and stress and the irrational behaviour of your stake-holders, management team and entire organisation, Chapter 3 tells you how to work on your resilience as a (transformational) leader. You will need this if we look at the magnitude and expected duration of the economic tsunami building up.

Then I will tell you about the practical method I developed to Fix, Reset and Accelerate a business in twelve months. I will share with you a holistic model to help you get to the core issues fast, the pitfalls to avoid during the turnaround, the three phases to take your business through and the seven key building blocks you need for business turnaround.

Chapters 5 to 10 will help you build the foundations of a sustainable turnaround for your business, which will immediately impact your profitability and strategic positioning. These building blocks discuss monitoring performance, business diagnosis, alignment of your management team, future vision (strategy, business model and earning model) and unleashing your talent (your company's core competitive advantage now and in future).

In Chapter 10 I include the turnaround DNA skills your team will need to help you improve profitability, reset strategy, business and earning model, and accelerate implementation to get to the (renewed) market faster than competitors.

In Chapter 11 I share with you the complete structure that I use for running my turnaround programmes, and that I constantly fine-tune to reflect the learnings from my projects.

The final chapter summarises the key takeaways. You can use this, together with Chapter 11, as a checklist on your journey and return to the relevant chapters when you need details.

At the end of the book you will find additional resources to support you during your turnaround journey.

My background

I have been working for over twenty-two years in business transformation, development and the rescue of failing companies, turning around businesses from losses to double-digit profit and growth within two years.

I am a business and strategy consultant; Turnaround CEO and member of the Turnaround Management Association (UK); a Rapid Transformational Therapist with the Marisa Peer Institute; an advisory board member of the Global Artificial Intelligence Forum; and I was positioned thirty-fourth on the board empowerment ranking in the Netherlands in 2016.

I am passionate about making company improvement sustainable, by building (future) inclusive and resilient leaders, who make a difference in the lives of others and a difference in the world.

My dream – my next big thing from the moment the pandemic hit – is to help as many businesses as I can (especially medium-sized businesses) to survive and thrive in difficult times, by making business rescue and transformation skills accessible for them. This book is the first step to achieving that dream. At the end of the book you will find what's next.

Thoughts become things. What you hold in your head, you hold in your hand: change your thoughts and you will change the outcomes of your business and personal life.

Remember (as Alan Watts said): 'The real you is not a puppet which life pushes around. The real, deep down you is the whole universe'.[2]

Go develop your people and change your business and, through that, make the world a better place.

---

2   Alan Watts, 'The Real You', www.youtube.com/watch?v=m MRrCYPxD0I

PART ONE
HANDLING ALL-PERVASIVE CHANGE AND CRISIS

1

What Is Happening In The World And How Do We Deal With It?

At the time of writing, we are still reeling from the effects of the COVID-19 pandemic and its impact on our local and global economies. We might never fully understand how we got here or be certain who the heroes and villains of this story are. Given the severity of the aftermath, it is much wiser to focus on what you can control, which is how to get your company out of this mess, and help it not only survive but thrive in this absurd new reality.

Let's become investigators. Finding and understanding the facts, based on published trusted information from global intergovernmental organisations, policy makers and transnational co-operations, is the start of our empowering journey. Then let's collate this information to answer the following questions:

- What is really happening (at global, local and company levels)?

- What is going to happen in the future?

- What do companies need to do to come out of this as winners?

What is really happening?

Prevention and recovery health measures have been set up by the World Health Organization (WHO). Parallel to that, financial measures were developed by the International Monetary Fund (IMF) to limit the human and economic impact of the pandemic. The World Economic Forum (WEF) also started to push the Great Reset agenda, combined with the Fourth Industrial Revolution.

Corporate philanthropists started getting involved in funding research, solutions and policy-making. The European Union gained strength during the pandemic in Europe, with member states communicating about coordinated global measures and referring to global experts in their speeches.

The public continues voicing its opinion at government responses to the crisis via social media and social unrest is on the rise. Global cooperation is also increasing as there is a common conviction that we are all sharing the same (health) pool. Co-ordination seems to be required to prevent some people urinating in the pool while others are trying to swim in it.

As local policy makers try to carry out the global bodies' guidelines, lockdowns have crippled economies and caused a drop in exports. Governments have offered support packages to businesses, pre-funded by the IMF, but this will need to be repaid from tax money and probably pushed to future generations.

The support packages are limited only to fixed cost and have decreased over time; they have barely cushioned the fall. The impact of the decline in demand and export will be absorbed by the businesses, themselves with zero support.

With the current economic developments and (progressive) lockdowns, business owners and leaders are being confronted with three key problems that are severely impacting their businesses:

- **Shrinking markets and lower revenues, while capacity is still fixed.** Government support does not typically cover decline in demand and export. With expected further decline in the economy in 2021, an increasing number of companies worked in 2020 to prepare or implement layoffs.

- **With employees in lockdown, companies are unable to remotely manage their operations; managing people moved overnight from control-based to trust-based management.** Businesses can't also keep a closer watch over the wellbeing and mental health of their employees amid a pervasive health crisis. This increases uncertainty and the risk of discontinuity of their operations. Working from home is becoming the forced norm and is likely to continue through 2021 for many businesses.

- **Companies have had to shift towards digital.** This means remote working, cloud storage, cloud computing, big data and e-commerce. The companies that stayed in business up to the end of 2020 were those already skilled in these areas and agile enough to make this shift. However, most have focused on survival in their move to digital and have not considered the long-term solutions that will gain them competitive advantage. They have not changed their business models and earning models or adopted impactful technology such as robotics, artificial intelligence and 3D printing.

What is going to happen in the future?

To answer this, we must look to the real influencers in the global arena who are currently shaping the future. If we leave the philanthropists out of it and focus on institutionalised global bodies, the list will include:

- The International Monetary Fund (IMF)
- The United Nations (UN), including the World Health Organization (WHO)
- The World Economic Forum (WEF)

Let us look at these key global influencers in turn: their members, their mission and the developments they are driving. Before we step in and investigate, I note that humanity is good and that most intentions are positive, but sometimes greed enters the game for individuals or countries and things take a negative turn. The only way to reverse that course is to collectively understand the global shifts, get involved and contribute to ensuring that change will be for good. Sitting back and condemning will not get humanity far.

The International Monetary Fund

The IMF is an international organisation of 190 member countries, formed in 1944 and headquartered in Washington, DC. Its objectives are to promote international monetary cooperation, international trade, high employment, exchange-rate stability, sustainable economic growth and making resources available to member countries in financial difficulty, while periodically depending on the World Bank for its resources.

Besides gathering and analysing data, the IMF monitors its members' economies and directs policies for improvement. The IMF has recently incorporated the WHO's COVID-19 indicators in its economic monitoring models, as the pandemic is now a major driver for economic decline.

Regarding the COVID-19 pandemic, the IMF said in 2020:

> 'The Great Lockdown will be the worst economic downturn since the Great Depression of 1929. The global economy's long ascent back to pre-pandemic levels of activity will remain prone to setbacks. It will be difficult to rekindle economic activity, while the pandemic is still surging.'[3]

The United Nations

The UN is an intergovernmental organisation with 193 members consisting of sovereign states. It was established after World War II with the aim of preventing future wars. Its goals are: maintaining international peace and security; protecting human rights; delivering humanitarian aid; promoting sustainable development; upholding international law; developing friendly relations among nations; achieving

---

3   'Press Conference: World Economic Outlook, January 2021 update', www.imf.org/external/mmedia/view.aspx? vid=6225429936001

international cooperation; and being a centre for harmonising the actions of nations. It is the largest, most familiar, most internationally represented and most powerful intergovernmental organisation in the world.

The UN system includes a multitude of specialised agencies, such as the World Bank Group, the World Health Organization (WHO), the World Food Programme, UNESCO and UNICEF. The programmes and funds are financed through voluntary rather than assessed contributions, hence the active role of philanthropy.

The United Nations Sustainable Development Goals were adopted by all UN member states in 2015, as a universal call to action to end poverty, protect the planet and ensure that all people enjoy peace and prosperity by 2030. These goals are being implemented, monitored and reported upon to the United Nations.

The seventeen global goals are:[4]

1. No poverty

2. Zero hunger

3. Good health and wellbeing

4. Quality education

5. Gender equality

---

4   UN Sustainable Development Goals, www.un.org/sustainable development/sustainable-development-goals

6. Clean water and sanitation

7. Affordable and clean energy

8. Decent work and economic growth

9. Industry innovation and infrastructure

10. Reduced inequalities

11. Sustainable cities and communities

12. Responsible consumption and production

13. Climate action

14. Life below water

15. Life on land

16. Peace, justice and strong institutions

17. Partnerships for goals

The United Nations' take on COVID-19:

> 'COVID-19 is having a devastating
> impact on all 17 goals and threatening the
> achievements already made in many years.
> While the virus has impacted everyone, it
> is the poorest and most vulnerable who are
> affected disproportionally by the pandemic...
> To recover from the COVID-19 pandemic, we
> must put people at the centre of the response to
> achieve more equitable and resilient outcomes
> for all. The SDGs and the Paris Agreement are
> our compass to a transformative recovery, that

reduces the risk of future crises and brings the inclusive and sustainable development.'[5]

The World Health Organization

The WHO, the health arm of the United Nations, was established in 1948, with the objective of the attainment by all people of the highest possible level of health. Health is defined by the WHO as a 'state of complete physical, mental and social wellbeing and not merely the absence of illness or infirmity'.[6] The WHO is governed by 192 member states through the World Health Assembly, whose main tasks are to approve the WHO programme and budget for the following two years and to decide major policy questions.

The WHO's take on COVID-19:[7]

'WHO is hopeful that countries will use targeted interventions where and when needed, based on the local situation. We well understand the frustration that many people, communities and governments are feeling as the pandemic drags on, and as cases rise again.

---

5   UN Department of Economic and Social Affairs (DESA), 'Achieving SDGs in the wake of COVID-19', September 2020, www.un-ilibrary. org/content/papers/27081990
6   UN Constitution, www.who.int/about/who-we-are/constitution
7   World Health Organization, 'WHO Director-General opening remarks and audio file for COVID-19 press briefing 12 October 2020', thenewsmarket.com, 2020, www.thenewsmarket.com/news/who-director-general-s-opening-remarks-and-audio-file-for-covid-19-press-briefing-12-october--2020/s/1fd152e3-575e-4fdf-b075-2ec4ec11b76a

There are no shortcuts, and no silver bullets.
The answer is a comprehensive approach,
using every tool in the toolbox.'

The WHO is working with philanthropists and other health organisations on the Access to COVID-19 Tools (ACT) Accelerator. With this initiative they want to speed up the search for an effective vaccine for all countries, support the building of manufacturing capabilities and buy supplies ahead of time so that two billion doses can be fairly distributed by the end of 2021.

The World Economic Forum[8]

The WEF was set up in 1971. It is renowned for its yearly meeting in Davos (Switzerland) in which the world's top influential leaders from politics, business, civil society, academia, the media and the arts take part. In 2020, nearly 3,000 participants from 117 countries were present, including fifty-three heads of state. The WEF is the most influential global platform in the world. Its chairman Klaus Schwab has published two influential books: *The Fourth Industrial Revolution*[9] and *COVID-19: The Great Reset*.[10] These two books have led to, and are still engendering, further research, publications, policy developments and pilots.

---

8   Based a multitude of publications and interviews produced by the WEF, www.weforum.org
9   K Schwab, *The Fourth Industrial Revolution* (Random House, 2017)
10   K Schwab, *COVID-19: The Great Reset* (Forum, 2020)

The WEF's take on COVID-19 is: 'The pandemic represents a rare but narrow window of opportunity to reflect, reimagine, and reset our world.'[11] When the founder of the WEF says Great Reset, he really means radically changing the world and creating a new normal. The Fourth Industrial Revolution will be the main driver of change. The Fourth Industrial Revolution and Great Reset are being translated into policy documents and implemented by global bodies, so it's important to understand what these two phenomena mean at the global and local levels. This is essential for the future of every company.

The aftermath of the COVID-19 crisis will be political, economic and social disruptions. Inconsistencies, inadequacies and contradictions are being brought to light in multiple systems (health, financial, political, energy and education) and are exposed by this global health crisis. Countries, industries and communities are and will be facing complex challenges.

The Fourth Industrial Revolution (the digital transformation) has been speeded up by the lockdowns. Life as we knew it (learning, work, shopping, worship, collaboration) has been redefined. Being successful has now become dependent on the ability to use technology to generate value and experiences.

---

11   K Schwab, 'Now is the time for a Great Reset', www.weforum.org, www.weforum.org/agenda/2020/06/now-is-the-time-for-a-great-reset

The WEF published research on the future of jobs in October 2020, to examine how business leaders are reacting globally to the COVID-19 pandemic and how they are using the Fourth Industrial Revolution to ensure business continuity.[12] The findings were as follows:

Planned business measures in response to COVID-19

Accelerate the digitisation of work processes	84%
Offer opportunities to work remotely	83%
Accelerate automation of tasks	50%
Accelerate the digitisation of upskilling/reskilling	42%
Accelerate the implementation of upskilling/reskilling programmes	35%
Accelerate ongoing organisational transformation	34%
Temporarily reassign workers to different tasks	30%
Temporarily reduce workforce	28%
Permanently reduce workforce	13%
Temporarily increase workforce	5%
No specific measures implemented	4%
Permanently increase workforce	1%

After the steam engine, electricity and information technology (the sources of the first three industrial revolutions) comes the Fourth Industrial Revolution, our current potential for connectivity, which is eliminating the barriers between the physical, digital and

---

12 'The Future of Jobs Report 2020', World Economic Forum, 2020, www.weforum.org/reports/the-future-of-jobs-report-2020

biological worlds and changing how we live, work and relate to one another.

This Fourth Industrial Revolution is unprecedented in the scale, scope, complexity and speed of its impact on our systems of production, management and governance and the unpredictability of its outcomes. It is evolving at an exponential rate, disrupting almost every industry in every country.[13]

Combine billions of people connected by mobile devices with an exponential increase in processing power, availability of data and storage capacity, access to knowledge and emerging technology (such as artificial intelligence, robotics, the internet of things, autonomous vehicles, 3D printing, nanotechnology, biotechnology, materials science, energy storage and quantum computing) and you get dazzling outcomes and breakthroughs. These include algorithms that predict behavioural choices and events to an increased symbiosis between micro-organisms, our bodies, the products we consume and even the buildings we inhabit.

Due to the increase of internet coverage and mobile use, the Fourth Industrial Revolution is opening new markets and creating global consumers. At the supply side, it will increase efficiency and productivity, decrease transportation and communication costs and

---

13 Based a multitude of publications and interviews produced by the WEF, www.weforum.org

make logistics and global supply chains more effective, reducing the overall cost of trade. It will remove the constraints of physical location and give technology entrepreneurs access to capital, talent, networks and other resources.

Alongside this great potential for development come great risks. Global income levels will improve the quality of life for some populations. Innovators, shareholders and investors are expected to flourish. But as technology replaces and reshapes jobs, traditional labour will be displaced. If well managed, the Fourth Industrial Revolution can lead to a net increase in safe and rewarding jobs, but if badly managed it will breed greater inequality, dissatisfaction and unfairness, and social unrest. Inequality represents the greatest societal concern associated with the Fourth Industrial Revolution.

The WEF is aware that the response to manage this revolution must be integrated and comprehensive, involving all stakeholders of the global policy: public and private sectors, academia and civil society.

Even the most informed and best-connected CEOs and senior business executives are finding the acceleration of innovation and the velocity of disruption hard to comprehend, predict or anticipate. The customer demand is shifting towards mobile living, due to growing transparency and consumer engagement. The way services and products are designed, marketed and delivered will need to be re-examined.

The industrial revolution is giving access to global digital platforms for research, development, marketing, sales and distribution to new entrants. New entrants are changing how products and services are offered, delivered and serve unmet needs. They are disrupting existing industry value chains and competing on quality, speed and price.

Technology-enabled platforms combining demand and supply are disrupting entire industries. They are combining smartphones, involvement of people, assets and data to create entirely new ways of distributing goods and services.

Companies will be able to know more about clients through data and analytics. They will have more customers to serve and can adjust service to them based on AI algorithms and enhanced experience. Products and services will be enhanced with digital capabilities to add more value. Assets will be more durable and resilient as they can be monitored and timely maintained. New forms of collaboration will rise, global platforms will emerge and, with them, new business models.

The Fourth Industrial Revolution will converge physical, digital and biological worlds and generate increased complexity for governments. COVID-19 is showing already that the majority of legislators, regulators and governments are unable to cope with the rapid pace of change, access to information and the impact of the Fourth Industrial Revolution.

Citizens are and will be increasingly engaging like never before with governments; they voice their opinions, coordinate their efforts and circumvent the supervision of public authorities. Social unrest will push governments to change how they engage the public in policy-making and decision-making. Top-down decision-making will no longer work. Meanwhile, governments have increased access to pervasive surveillance systems and the ability to control the digital infrastructure, and are increasing their control over the population.

If governments want to gain a competitive edge internationally, they will need to understand the Fourth Industrial Revolution and what they are regulating; become more agile, open to dialogue and collaborate closely with business and civil society; adopt new methods of dialogue and decision-making; and understand how to balance the interests of the public with supporting innovation and technological development.

The Fourth Industrial Revolution will offer possibilities to enhance humanity, but will also impact the sense of privacy, ownership, consumption patterns, work–life balance, personal development, careers, development of skills, socialising and building relationships. Debates about the loss of control over our data are expected to intensify, as will dialogue about ethical boundaries in the rise of human augmentation in the areas of health, cognition and capabilities.

What do companies need to do to come out of this as winners?

Step up and show up

As humans we always have control. We are responsible for directing evolution by how we show up as citizen, consumer or investor. To turn the Fourth Industrial Revolution and the Great Reset into a force for good, we need to step up and start to take part in shaping a future of purpose-led, inclusive, sustainable and trustworthy leadership that enhances humanity (instead of robotising it and enslaving it), a future that balances economic profit and societal value for everyone and promotes the wellbeing of mankind and preservation of the planet.

Align with the environment

Companies will need to equip themselves with the know-how to understand and act upon these shifts and their impact on performance, to align their strategies and capital allocation with drivers for long-term value creation, and strengthen their preparedness and resilience to crisis and environmental shocks. Immersion in the digital economy will be vital, as it will play a crucial role in the post-COVID economic recovery.

Adapt the business model

The Fourth Industrial Revolution will change the fabric of businesses in terms of customer expectations and interaction, product/service characteristics, role and innovation in the supply chain, and business and earning model. Being an established brand, with a good customer base, lean processes, good sales and marketing interface, is no longer a guarantee for success. Added value, business model, earning model and role in the supply chain will need to be re-examined strategically in order to be able to survive and thrive during this Great Reset, driven by the Fourth Industrial Revolution.

Companies must move towards collaborative models and combined goals, in terms of value and purpose, and invest in culture and new leadership capabilities. The result will be a digitally intelligent enterprise and ecosystem that are nimble, resilient, distributed and adaptive to disruptive change.

Talent and leadership

Talent, leadership, culture and structures will have to be rethought. Companies will need to re-examine the way they do business. Business leaders and senior executives must work to understand the Fourth Industrial Revolution, monitor their changing environment, reassess with their teams how they are doing business, and continuously innovate and adjust their process to survive and thrive in these changing times.

Talent, more than capital, will become businesses' most important asset. Shortages in talent can be expected in the market. Businesses will need to continuously develop their own (extended) teams.

Education of the leadership and talent needs to focus on capabilities to effectively interact and execute in ecosystems, and deliver new value on developing entrepreneurial talent and mindset as well as the adaptation and transformation skills needed to keep up with the speed of this industrial revolution. Top-down decision-making will no longer work. Businesses need agile and human-centric collaboration models.

Role of the small and medium enterprise

Small and medium enterprises (SMEs) across Europe will get special attention from governments and policy makers as they employ more than 50% of the working population and heavily contribute to rebuilding the economy and generating new solutions after recessions. They will face funding challenges in accessing the new technologies that will drive the Fourth Industrial Revolution, as they are operating in markets with heavily funded corporates. Global policy makers will be incrementally urging SMEs (from 2021 onwards) to take a leading role in policy developments, to ensure that they are offered solutions that will help them solve real-life problems.

Summary

In this chapter we discussed what is really happening in the world at global, local and business levels, predicted what is going to happen in the future, and highlighted what companies need to do to come out of this pandemic as winners.

You need to:

- Step up and engage in the Great Reset and Fourth Industrial Revolution

- Align your company to its changing environment

- Adapt your business model and earning model

- Invest in the development of your leadership and team

- Get involved in the policy-making process and solutions if you are an SME

In the coming chapter I will tell you how these developments could adversely impact your business and what you need to do to reverse this and thrive.

2
What Happens In All-Pervasive Change And Crisis?

Between now and 2030 we will live through all-pervasive change. This chapter will examine what that means to businesses and the people who depend on them, the shape our journey will take and the signposts we should be looking out for.

The economic crisis generated by the COVID-19 pandemic and subsequent lockdowns is unprecedented in nature. It has been compared by the IMF to the Great Depression in its economic outlook, as in 2020.[14] The lockdowns in 2020 and 2021 keep economies stuck in recession; the IMF forecasted growth in 2021 and 2022,

---

14 G Gopinath, 'The Great Lockdown: Worst economic downturn since the Great Depression', IMFBlog, https://blogs.imf.org/2020/04/14/the-great-lockdown-worst-economic-downturn-since-the-great-depression

but made this contingent on the effectiveness, availability, coverage and speed of vaccination across the globe. Given the impact of the recession, the Fourth Industrial Revolution and Great Reset, a fast recovery and return to normal and the level of prosperity before the crisis is not a valid option. The future between 2021 and 2030 is being redefined and its shape is not one that is familiar.

The indicators of an economic crisis are as follows: the Gross Domestic Product (GDP) drops, the yield curve (interest rates on bonds) inverts, unemployment rises, consumer confidence in the economy drops and the Leading Economic Index (LEI) (which indicates the overall health of the economy and businesses) deteriorates.

A recession follows when inflation or deflation kicks in, assets (real estate and stock) lose value, consumption of services and goods drops, and other economic activity slows down because of the declining demand. This has a devastating impact on the viability of businesses and on people's livelihoods. As individuals lose their jobs and therefore, possibly, their homes and the ability to provide for themselves and their families, their mental health suffers. Constant media coverage of the recession leads to more fear and anxiety.

Entrepreneurs navigating the post-pandemic economy will have to deal with shifting business models and marketplaces next to the impact of economic decline and recession. They will either adapt, survive and thrive or fail to adjust and cease to exist.

It is these entrepreneurs who rebuild an economy after a crisis, in particular the owners and leaders of medium-sized businesses. These are the people who are always looking for opportunities to build a business, create jobs and grow the economy. New opportunities are born every day at the heart of every recession.

Entrepreneurs who have sound business sense are not crushed by a crisis; they look for opportunities and plan how to convert them. It helps to remember that many of the greatest businesses were by-products of a recession; they gave customers what they really needed, added value during the economic crisis and because of that managed to thrive when the economy recovered.

In this chapter we will look at how companies get into crisis mode, how a collective shift in perception is the key to recovery, and how companies can be pulled out of a crisis. Let's get you the required insights to Fix, Reset and Accelerate your business, claim your turf and be a winner in this new economic reality.

The turnaround DNA

First I want to tell you why I care about crisis manage-ment and company rescue – why it is in my DNA.

I have worked for over twenty-two years in business transformation and rescuing failing companies. To date I have worked with thirty-five companies across fourteen industries. I became deeply curious about piecing together the puzzle of company crisis, company rescue and recovery. I wanted to understand how companies get in a crisis, and how I could pull them out of it as quickly as possible to increase their chances of recovery and improve the lives of people in the company. Every project and organisation, company owner and business leader I worked with helped me to discover more.

There is something in my DNA that makes a highly stressful situation resonate with me. I grew up in Casablanca, as the youngest of two children. My parents were idealists, working to make others' lives better. They were authority figures, at the top of their game; Mom was a teacher (with four classes of more than thirty-five children per year, building future generations) and Dad was a police investigator, solving serious crimes and bringing the villains to justice. I admired his ferocity. Seeing him reacting in stressful situations was awesome.

I grew up in a male-dominated culture. To earn your rank in the pack, you had to do well at school, win at (boys') sports, accept scary challenges like jumping from high places and climbing trees, and be a force to be reckoned with at street fights. To be one of the guys, I had to be their mental and physical equal. When I was between five and seven, I would make myself block the fear while watching scary Alfred Hitchcock movies with my older brother that he had dared me to watch, but still secretly checking underneath the bed before sleeping.

Growing up in that environment, I knew that to get ahead you have to dream big, push boundaries, show up and speak up. You have to walk into what scares you most and just do it. I learned that when you stay calm in the face of terror, you can think clearly, you can stay safe and everything gets better in the end; there is a present wrapped in sandpaper in every situation, and if we are patient enough and calm enough we will find it and become better because of it. With this attitude, I took on challenges, said yes to difficult and scary stuff and made it a sport to get out my comfort zone. This made me best in my class at the university school (the Ecole Universitaire de Technologie) and brought me to the Netherlands on an exchange programme.

My first job at twenty-two was with a US company in the Netherlands. At first glance, I looked like a young girl, eager to learn and perform. I was also fierce. I said yes to projects that others turned down because they were intellectually challenging, too complex, risky or with difficult managers and teams. My attitude was: bring it on. I worked hard, calculated risks, thought everything through, was never intimidated (or at least not for long), always built a strong tribe to make change happen, rebounded after a fall, helped others achieve in my footsteps and always got the job done.

I started as a code trouble-shooter fixing critical applications; working in new product development with tight deadlines; solving complex problems with processes, organisations and teams; and doing kamikaze implementation projects with scary deadlines. Before I knew it, I was being directed towards transformation work in a crisis environment. People who had worked with me told others when they came across a frightening project: 'Talk to her, she will do it.'

Ten years later, aged thirty-two, I fell in love with company rescue and turnaround management while working as a margin improvement director for a large firm. Profits were dropping and the company almost making losses when I was asked to run a one-year programme to help turn the company round and get it to a safer place.

I set up a programme team and reported to one of the greatest and most humane leaders I have ever worked with. We worked hard as a team, had fun and brought, collectively, the ship safely back to harbour. I decided that this was what I was here for: building and developing (young) leaders and taking them on a mission to rescue and develop companies.

What do I like about this work? It is always nearly impossible, challenging, high adrenaline and high impact. It requires thinking on your feet, doing something that matters. You can develop awesome leaders and form great teams (your pack). And it is awesome when you pull it together: moving a company from losses (and risk of collapsing and making people redundant) to a huge profit and success in a short period of time; and knowing that you really made it, against all odds, and that the company is safe. If you wanted to be a superhero as a kid, this is your chance. It is an indescribable high.

How companies get into a crisis

A crisis in a company usually starts with something happening outside the company that impacts its earning capacity. The company is still in a comfortable state, so does not realise that the game has changed and does not react adequately or swiftly enough. The consequences are top-line issues: costs becoming too high, profitability decreasing, stress in the leadership and management layer spreading to the workforce and, shortly after, issues with stakeholders (employee representatives, clients, suppliers, shareholders, banks and supervisors).

By then, the organisation and its leadership are in a crisis, and organisational pathologies start developing.[15] The organisation gets stuck in survival mode.

15 RM Kanter, 'Leadership and the psychology of turnarounds', *Harvard Business Review*, 2003, June; 81(6):58–67, 136

To really survive, the organisation needs to be moved out of that state as quickly as possible – through targeted interventions – because the solvency and the continuity of the company are at risk.

How a collective perception shift is key to recovery

When a company crisis becomes a fact and the bad news is shared, the isolation among executives starts, followed by denial, then by blaming or avoiding one another. Silos replace the supply chain and managers begin to copy the leaders by disliking, avoiding or even sabotaging one another. People start hiding information and denying responsibility. Important meetings are cancelled or postponed.

Employees' workloads and the psychological pressures on them increase. Trust and engagement decrease, absenteeism and staff turnover rise and the cost of replacing staff increases. Employees pour time and energy into protecting themselves rather than focusing on joint problem-solving. Managers and employees enter a stage of learned helplessness. They feel there is nothing they can do to make a difference to the company's fortune, so they become passive and stick to the nine to five; they do their work, play it safe and go home.

The company then enters a collective state of ignorance, one in which everybody pretends not to know what is happening and carries on like nothing has happened. These organisational pathologies reinforce one another and the company enters a death spiral. Reversing this dynamic requires not only a company turnaround but, more importantly, a psychological turnaround.

A psychological turnaround starts with a perception shift, when a leader normalises what is happening and shows that no one goes through life without struggles, and that a company crisis is just one of them. That every struggle we encounter is simply a mirror to help us improve and move forward; to get us to reassess how we are leading; to help us rethink the future of the company and move it towards a healthier state and a sustainable and successful future.

A leader should show people that amid the struggle and crisis, they need to find the spirit and strength to embrace the truth without ego, get up again and do whatever it takes to rise stronger. In (personal and company) turnarounds and transformations, the one who is willing to be the most uncomfortable will make the greatest impact. Leaning into discomfort is imperative. That means entering the process with eyes wide open (for the facts, data and new answers), dealing with what emerges and wholeheartedly embracing themselves as human beings (with flaws and imperfections) but, above all, as brave leaders and change-makers who will get the problem fixed.

How companies can be pulled out of a crisis

A company crisis and turnaround are when leadership matters most. To pull the company from its downward spiral, leaders need to move the organisation from a state of collective ignorance, passivity and helplessness to one of ownership, engagement and the willingness and ability to move the organisation towards a better future.

The only way a leader can reverse a company's decline is to rewire its collective beliefs by re-empowering people. This means stopping the secrecy and denial and insisting on dialogue; removing blame and insisting on respect; removing avoidance and turf protection and insisting on collaboration; and by replacing passivity and helplessness with new knowledge, skills, involvement and initiative. This psychological turnaround needs to take place alongside the company turnaround.

Pulling the company out of a crisis is an act of leadership. It requires a positive attitude, resilience and never giving up on the company and its employees. It takes three to six months to stop the downward spiral (the Fix phase). In this period you will have to deal with the worries and pressures of your team, employees, shareholders, banks, employee representatives, clients, suppliers, market supervisors and media. You will be facing a full-blown storm, irrational fear-based behaviour and hostility, and you will be working between sixty and eighty hours a week.

Getting a grip on your company will not be easy, but it is feasible if you:

- Keep calm and collected and push forward.

- Show clear, strong but empathic leadership.

- Eradicate office politics and create safety and trust for employees.

- Analyse and understand the root causes of the issues.

- Stop the bleeding quickly and stabilise the business.

- Move fast with vigilance.

- Engage, energise and develop your employees to get them unstuck and moving towards recovery.

- Engage all stakeholders and turn them into mentors and sponsors.

- Dare to take tough decisions in a respectful and honourable way.

- Rethink your business model and define the company's future.

- Don't stay too long in the bunker. Get out, interact and connect.

- Take care of you. Set up some objective counselling for yourself from a buddy or mentor so you will have a safe space to decompress.

Once the crisis is in hand and the company is back on track, your job is not over; the turnaround and transformation will need to continue. Ensure that you stay sane, centred, fit and emotionally available at work and at home. In the next chapter we will discuss how you can do this.

Leadership development, empowerment and dialogue

In my projects, the most effective methods for pulling companies out of crisis have proved to be a focused development programme (for executives, management and talent) and targeted executive coaching. Alongside this, initiating group dialogue has been necessary to heal the collective trauma that emerges from the organisational pathologies of the crisis.

I am not a fan of vague cultural change programmes that take months and lead nowhere. To build a sustainable and successful future, companies need empowerment and a transformation programme for the business leader, his executive team managers and talent to create the 'hero army'. Parallel to that, a targeted organisation-wide shift is required from crisis towards inclusion, involvement, paced problem-solving and healthier dynamics.

Impact on (mental) health

Leading an organisation during times of crisis, running a business rescue programme and managing dialogues, usually in a hostile environment, generate great uncertainty for leaders and their organisations. In times of uncertainty, the human body will experience persistent stress and will unconsciously linger too long in action mode. The sympathetic system will remain active and will enable us to survive in these threatening situations: to fight, to flee and to perform with a high heart rate, high blood pressure and fast breathing. Getting stuck in this 'fight or flight' state prevents the body from experiencing physical relaxation, repair, regeneration and recovery. The result is burnout.

During times of great uncertainty, we are confronted with the emergence of old programming (beliefs, imprints and traumas) which could trigger self-doubt, anxiety, performance anxiety, fear of public speaking, depression and sometimes phobias. The body will then be accelerating with the brakes on, which is exhausting and ineffective for oneself, the task at hand and our direct environment (at home as well as at work). Taking a timely day off and working on getting unstuck and seeking a fresh perspective on issues with a mentor or buddy is a must for restoring balance, for keeping healthy and resilient, and for going back to manage the company rescue and turnaround with even stronger beliefs and stamina.

When I started working on transformations and business rescue, I was confronted with irrational behaviours in companies, high levels of stress, getting stuck in 'do' mode, not being able to relax or sleep and old programmings, all of which emerge in hostile situations. In 2015 I was hospitalised for nearly a week with a neurological dysfunction and could not move without a wheelchair for a month. I will never know for sure if this was caused by my kite surfing accident six months earlier or by high levels of stress, but I did know that I needed a way to deal with the stress generated by my work to stay healthy and sane.

During this episode I kept working but for fewer hours. I did more through my team (my pack). I sorted out how to work on my recovery and developed new resilience and success habits that I still use. I recovered in six months and started helping my team and later my clients to adopt these habits. In the next chapter I will tell you more about these resilience and success habits, which will help you through your company's rescue or transformation period.

Summary

After setting the scene about what is going to happen between 2020 and 2030 in the first chapter, we discussed in this chapter how a company gets into a crisis, how a collective perception shift is key to recovery and how companies can be pulled out of a crisis.

I explained that stopping the downward spiral of your company will take three to six months (the Fix phase) followed by an additional six months for Reset and then Accelerate. You will need to keep going until it is done. For that you will need resilience and success habits that will help you to keep going. In the next chapter I will tell you the what and how of these success and resilience habits.

3

Resilience For Leading In All-Pervasive Change And Crisis

You need resilience to lead your company through tough times: the three to six months you will need to stop the downward spiral, plus another six months to reset the company and accelerate it. Resilience will keep you performing at the top of your game and developing the right team and organisation to accompany you on your journey. Leaders who do not have resilience behave destructively and create toxic professional relationships. The toxicity trickles down and infects the entire organisation. A sick workplace will not help you achieve the change you want to see.

Resilient leaders are:

- **Mission-driven:** they are aware of their raison d'être and have enough personal and professional grit to make it happen. They are focused and loyal to their dreams, they work hard, don't give up in the face of hardship and make things happen.

- **Whole human beings:** they live with an open heart, with passion and empathy. They see and listen to people around them and inspire these skills in others.

- **Balanced:** they are physically, mentally, emotionally and spiritually balanced and resilient. They sustain and recover their energy under stress and they can go through major events, even traumas, without engaging in dysfunctional behaviour (harming self or others).

- **Centred:** they balance bonding and autonomy and don't allow negative events or people to define or break them.

- **Adaptable:** they can deal with uncertainty and change and manage adversity, challenges, setbacks and traumatic situations without being destroyed by them.

- **Caring:** they look beyond themselves, making sure their teams also stay in flow and energised. This creates healthy workplace dynamics and minimises conflict and burnout.

There are four prerequisites for resilient leadership: knowing who you really are, knowing why you are here (your mission or purpose in life), understanding and dealing with what can hold you back, and knowing the success principles and habits you need to follow to become and stay resilient. In this chapter I will tell you how to achieve all of this using the tools I have found most effective.

Knowing who you really are

Through working with more than 1,000 people across a range of countries, companies, environments and situations, I have discovered that everybody has something unique about them. When you hear a person's stories about their childhood, upbringing, relationships, failures, successes and so on, you start to understand how their character has been built and how this contributes to who they are. But you also see that they are often unable to acknowledge their own worth because it has been buried under what is holding them back (failures, conditioning, pain, self-doubt and the fear of not being good enough). Ask someone to talk about a subject they are passionate about and something in them starts shining and, for a moment, everything that is holding them back collapses and you see them in all their glory. I always feel humbled when I have the opportunity to meet people at this point.

What I love about my work is finding greatness in people, making them see it and guiding them to free themselves from the ghosts of their past, which now have no power over them. Everyone is talented at something. When we are doing the exact thing we are talented at, we feel good, energised and happy. We excel, we shine. It feels easy and effortless. Einstein was meant to solve complex problems, Picasso was meant to paint, Rachmaninov was meant to play the piano. They found their talent and excelled at it.

You too are unique and extremely good at something. Maybe you have already discovered your talent. If not, it is easy to discover. You might have heard of the Myers-Briggs Type Indicator (MBTI), the best known and most trusted personality assessment on the market, backed up by seventy years of science-based research. This indicator helps you define your profile, noting your talents and how you see and interact with the world. It gives you insights into your talent and what motivates and drives you.

I took the MBTI test with my first employer when I was twenty-two, and I was amazed at the insights it delivered. It provided me with a great indication of my signature (what makes me unique) and a strong foundation for my personal development and growth. I have been using this method ever since for scouting and coaching talent in my business transformation and rescue work. I have still not found a better assessment tool.

You can take the assessment on the MBTI Institute website: www.mbtionline.com. It will take fifteen to twenty minutes and cost you around $50 for a detailed report with your personality indicator to be emailed to you.

I love to watch people read their indicator for the first time and understand why they are good at some things and terrible at others, and then to see them start excelling once they move towards jobs and activities that match their signature. They will tell you that, looking back, they understood why they felt so good when acting within their signature. Something held them back: doubt, bad feedback on their first steps, fear of not being able to earn money with what they are talented in.

Move towards your unique signature, understand yourself and find the source of your personal power, which will give you an inner sense of who you are. Your past, good or bad, was meant to build your greatness, and to give you what you need today to serve your calling.

Knowing your raison d'être

Building resilience is essential but our end goal must be to be happy in life. We want to thrive, not merely exist. We thrive and become happy in life when we pursue goals that are congruent with who we are, with our raison d'être.

The two key resources I have found useful for defining raison d'être are a book by Chin-Ning Chu, a leading philosopher and business strategist, and the Latifa meditation, a Sufi practice. I introduce my clients to these tools and, time after time, I am amazed by the results.

I came across Chin-Ning Chu's warrior philosophy twelve years ago. She is by far the best writer I have read on business strategy and resilience. She demonstrates how Asian philosophies can help us use the positive force hidden within us all to unleash our personal power. As Chin-Ning Chu states: 'By getting in touch with the power within you, you will gain unshakable clarity and focus to help you discover and achieve your intended destiny.'[16]

By reflecting on Chin-Ning Chu's insights, I came to understand that while we are all following a life path with many choices, there is a divine plan for each of us (our dharma or destiny). Our real goal in life is to use our talents to make a great contribution in the world before we die. Because our parents indoctrinated us with what they thought was right, it is likely that we have lost sight of our unique talent and our dharma. Life is a series of opportunities for discovery and learning, seeking who we are and why we are here.

16　C-N Chu, *Thick Face, Black Heart: The warrior philosophy for conquering the challenges of business and life* (Hachette, 1994)

To truly succeed in life and reach our dharma, we have to fully understand ourselves, become adaptable (so we don't crumple in times of change or crisis) and find a purpose beyond simply avoiding pain and pursuing pleasure. This means losing fear and finding our calling, mastering the art of detachment (what will be will be, and that is OK), believing in ourselves, seeing the oneness with the universe, seeing everything as perfect and accepting reality, pursuing wisdom from consciousness not virtue (for external approval), and working towards greatness.

I have also been supported in my journey towards my dharma by the Latifa meditation, an ancient Sufi guided meditation that was originally meant only to be practised by initiated disciples but now is accessible to everyone. Latifa is known as the journey back to yourself; it brings you into deep contact with your existence, desires, hope, trust, love and vitality. It helps you access what you want and to connect with your inner core, where you find your strength and peace. It brings you insight into the stuck emotions and beliefs that are holding you back and helps you release these emotions.

This meditation combines speaking the words of the Sufi meditation with hand movements over the Latifs, the six subtle centres of perception in the body. The Latifs lie dormant in everyone and awakening them is crucial for travelling back to our higher selves and connecting with our essence and our calling.

The Latifa meditation is a simple and powerful way to find the inner strength of purpose that will make you resilient in every aspect of your life.

When you practise the meditation regularly, it supports you in your quest for your dharma or destiny and calling, and helps you achieve transformation and sustainable change.

Go to the following link to access the Latifa meditation: https://answerinside.eu/Book-Giveaways

Understanding and dealing with what can hold you back

The three main factors that undermine our strength and hold us back from success and joy are how we experience and deal with stress, how we handle our emotions, and the limiting beliefs we have about ourselves (the result of old programming).

What happens when we are stressed

When we experience danger and become overwhelmed, we go outside our 'window of tolerance' and our limbic brain is switched on. We go into either the hyper-arousal zone (fight/flight) or the hypo-arousal zone (freeze). This means we cannot think 'straight' (or clearly), we dissociate (we don't see everything that is going on) and we release survival hormones.[17]

Change has become the new normal and the uncertainty that comes with change causes stress, so stress is also the new normal. Stress is not all bad if we understand it and can make it work for us. Research in neurology and psychology presented by Professor Kelly McGonigal in one of her lectures in 2015 has shown that we experience stress when things matter to us.[18] Stress generates hormones (neuro-steroids) that make our brains grow. Stress goes hand in hand with learning and growth, and it happens when we want to pursue positive and important things.

Stress can give us the sense of urgency we need to bring about change and move the company forward but it needs to be temporary. It should not turn into constant worry, sleepless nights and a drain on energy. Stress is only constructive when we are able to return to our window of tolerance at will. We need to understand stress, to talk about it openly, embrace and appreciate it as part of the change process, and help ourselves and others to deal with it if we want to achieve meaningful things.

Leaders have a social and moral responsibility to create human, healthy, happy and vibrant workplaces;

---

17 P Levine, *Waking the Tiger: Healing trauma* (North Atlantic Books, 2011)

18 K McGonigal, 'How to make stress your friend', 2013, www.ted. com/talks/kelly_mcgonigal_how_to_make_stress_your_friend

watch over their people and keep everyone's stress under control; promote resilience; and energise their teams. In times of change, leaders should work hand in hand with their talent management department/ HR, engaging in dialogue and communication about the change and having respectful and motivating conversations with employees about their wellbeing. Alongside the talent management department, leaders should monitor the levels of stress, trust, engagement, sickness and staff turnover in the organisation.

To make change successful and fun in your organisation, you need to build relationships with your people. Employees work hard for the leaders they respect and trust as humans, so be trustworthy. Give them what they need: meaningful work, support, a positive work environment and growth opportunities. Building a positive bond with your people is extremely rewarding. Meaningful relationships and bonds increase our confidence. We experience the tribe feeling, we feel safe and included, we feel connected, we show up, we engage in change, we become willing to take more responsibility and risk, we become energised, we experience less stress and we are happy at work.

How we deal with difficult emotions

When growing up, we learn that expressing good emotions is acceptable but that we should suppress and even avoid negative emotions. When negative emotions are denied and subdued, we suppress our life force energy (named Chi) and emotions spill over as disease. In Chinese medicine, diseases are caused or facilitated by trapped and unexpressed emotions and memories. The same principle holds for events and emotions that have been suppressed in an organisation.

During the transformation of any business, difficult decisions need to be taken: decisions that might involve letting colleagues go, stopping business lines, products or projects, and nullifying the efforts that people have made, possibly over years. Employees will experience loss, grief, failure and setbacks. Leaders need to be willing to talk openly, honestly and respectfully with their people about these events, addressing their own feelings and the collective feelings. Real leadership means opening your heart, showing empathy, listening and feeling, bringing your whole being to the table, and balancing bonding and autonomy.

This takes courage but it is worth it. In return you will receive trust, safety and a positive bond with your people. If you can turn difficult events into bonding opportunities and talk to your people about them, you will be able to heal together.

Emerging old programming and limiting beliefs

We saw above that when we move out of our window of tolerance because things really matter to us and we are threatened, our survival mechanisms (fight, flight or freeze) are activated. When events trigger old memories and related emotions, old negative beliefs (from our childhood) emerge. This often takes the form of the voice of a parent, teacher or family member saying 'Be careful', 'Don't bite off more than you can chew' or (the worst one) 'You can't do it anyway'. These voices and beliefs are stored in the subconscious mind.

You are not alone in this. We all have ugly childhood stories. Your ugly story is a present in sandpaper tied with razor wire: it looks bad, it looks ugly, you want to run away from it. But if you want to advance, you need to face the discomfort of unpacking it. When you see what's inside, the ghost of the story loses its power over you and you get your full personal power back.

When I work with clients, I see and hear their fear of their ugly story. When they share it and see that I am not shocked, that I have heard worse or that I can relate, I see their relief. These stories, stored in our subconscious, relate to events that made us feel unsafe, helpless, fearful, weak, incapable, not loveable or not enough. Usually these past events were not of our making, but inflicted on us. We do not need to feel shame about them, just healthy anger.

To find your voice, unleash your talent and identify your calling, you need to walk through your darkness, face your shadows and own your story. That's where real unshakable personal power comes from.

There are many therapeutic paths that you can use to take this journey. I have gained the results I need using a hypnotherapeutic technique, Marisa Peer's Rapid Transformational Therapy, which aims to help the client understand and release these limiting beliefs in one session of ninety minutes.[19] I am qualified to practise this technique and have been using it with clients to unleash their personal power.

Building and maintaining resilience

During a period of company rescue and all-pervasive change, we are focusing on immediate real-life problems such as saving jobs and creating a future for the company and its people. The temptation is to live more in our heads and forget to feel – to take care of everybody and everything else but forget ourselves. Our health is the price we pay for neglecting ourselves.

You need daily habits or drills to keep you centred, focused and working from your head and heart and staying present in your body. I will share with you here the practices and habits that I find effective for recovering quickly from stress, preserving my wellbeing and increasing my resilience.

---

19   M Peer, *Ultimate Confidence: The secrets to feeling great about yourself every day* (Sphere, 2009)

Choose from these habits the ones that resonate most with you; do them every day for twenty-one consecutive days and see how you feel. It takes one hour a day and has changed my life and that of my clients – and it can change yours.

Staying positive and believing you are enough

Your mind believes the words you tell it and the images you make in your head. Feed it positive images. I recommend you take a piece of paper and write on it the following words:

> Life is not perfect. We need to play and win
> with the cards we are dealt.
> Leave the pain of setbacks behind and decide
> how you will act next.
> All is well and all will be well, and whatever
> happens, you are worthy, you are loveable,
> you are capable and more than enough, and
> you are safe.

Keep this paper next to your bed and revisit it at the end of the day. You will need it during the company rescue and turnaround.

Visualising your dreams every day

What you hold in your head, you hold in your hands. When you believe that your dreams are possible and you are able to visualise them and feel thrilled about achieving them, that's what you start putting out into the universe every day and feel motivated to achieve. Top athletes see themselves winning in their head before they go out to win.

Living in the now (in a state of coherence)

Living in (or clinging to) the past causes depression; fearing the future causes anxiety. Together these are a recipe for a miserable day, week, month and life. Break the habit and live in the now. Let go, surrender, accept what is and trust that all is well and all will be well.

When you are in the here and now, you reach a state of coherence and flow. Your heart, mind and emotions are in energetic alignment and cooperation. You can start living in the now in only sixty seconds.

Here is a method to practise – you can do this seated. Breathe deeply three times, ground your feet (feel the four corners of your feet planted on the ground), become aware of all the sensations in your body and listen to the sounds in your environment for one minute. For the rest of the day, savour your coffee, feel the chair you are sitting on, feel the air on your skin as you walk, feel and observe the sunshine.

This feeling of being in the now extends to being present when you listen and are present with what you are doing. Living in the now and in a state of coherence will increase your mental focus, emotional stability and physical resilience. You will start enjoying life (and sensory experiences) while living, instead of staying stuck in your head.

Getting yourself back into the window of tolerance

We all experience moments when bad events, bad news and setbacks throw us off course, when we shift out of our window of tolerance. Learning how to get ourselves back into the window of tolerance is a bare necessity in crisis management and business rescue.

If you just have a few minutes, start with the 'living in the now' exercise above. Then soothe yourself: literally wrap your arms around yourself for as long as you need. Tell yourself you are loveable and capable and that you can handle this. If possible (if not in the moment of crisis, later the same day), talk to a mentor, buddy, loved one or friend. Work on regulating your emotions; get back in the here and now, look at your environment, feel and release your emotions, take care of you, practise positive thinking and remind yourself of the bigger picture – why you have chosen to do this job in the first place, that you are physically safe and that you will work this out.

Active meditation with the Silva Ultra Mind

Daily meditation is a key element of the resilience toolkit, and the most effective practice I have found is the active meditation of the Silva Ultra Mind method. I have been using it every day for ten years and always introduce my clients to it.

This method uses brain language (kinesthetic, visual and auditory thought processes) to help you reach a deeper state of relaxation of body and mind, centre yourself and learn to take control of your thought processes and the images you create in your head. This determines what you say to yourself and thereby how you feel (mentally and physically), how you relate to the world and how you perform. You can get results using this method for just twenty-one minutes a day. You will stop the overthinking that causes anxiety, improve your thoughts, health and mental faculties, and unleash your inner genius. It is one of the best tools for personal growth that I have found.

Go to the following link to access this active meditation: https://answerinside.eu/Book-Giveaways

Increasing the flow of your life force energy

High stress and related emotions lead to the stagnation of the life force energy; stagnation will lead to fatigue and, when it persists, to sickness. I have three trusted methods for keeping my energy flowing: at least one thirty-minute high-intensity workout a week; an hour of Qi Gong or dynamic yoga practice (Vinyasa flow) twice a week; and an acupuncture session when the first two don't help, or once a month for maintenance.

Mentors and meaningful connections

When working on solving a crisis, a company rescue or all-pervasive change, we get absorbed by the
process of planning and making things happen. We
disconnect from ourselves and others. Our work is
complex and stressful. It cannot be discussed with
family and friends at the dinner table. Objective counselling, in the form of a buddy or mentor whom you
trust, will help you to let off steam and decompress in
a safe space, organise your thoughts and get a fresh
perspective. Nurture these relationships and make
sure you pay forward what you take out.

This will give the required peace of mind to recon-
nect in a meaningful way with your loved ones, be
present and experience the comfort and protection of
your base.

Summary

After putting the above points into practice, go back
to the first two – who you really are and why you are
here – and reflect on how you express those in your
leadership. Do you want to be liked and trusted as a
leader? Be authentic; be who you really are in your
core, every day, everywhere and with everybody.
Authentic leaders are self-aware and genuine, they
know why they are here, they lead from the heart and
they make long-term impact; they make a difference.

Follow your heart and intuition. When you understand why you are here, you need to pursue it without fear and be prepared to pay the price to get there. Making a difference needs courage – saying yes in the face of the unknown.

You are not a puppet that life pushes around; you have in you the power that created worlds. Life is opportunity; the world around you is opportunity. Keep your eyes open to see that.

Work harder, make sacrifices and let your fear be your fuel. Never lose sight of what you want – go all in from the heart to achieve it. Seek guidance from experts, you don't need to walk the journey alone. You will make it and become not only successful but truly happy.

Company rescue is crucial for preserving jobs and creating a future for people and companies. More than ever, we need transformational leaders who are willing and able to rescue companies. Looking at the challenges of the post-2020 pandemic years, the Fourth Industrial Revolution in progress and the shifts in all industries, this will not be a sprint but a marathon. Transformational leaders will need resilience and grit, and in this chapter we discussed what resilience and grit mean and how to acquire them.

The first three chapters covered what is going to happen in the world, how companies respond to change and uncertainty and how leaders can develop the resilience and grit they need to face the challenges ahead. I will tell you in the next chapter how to Fix, Reset and Accelerate a business and make it thrive in twelve months.

PART TWO
METHODOLOGY

4

How To Fix, Reset And Accelerate Your Business In Twelve Months

When an organisation is underperforming, I see it as a sick patient who is losing blood (in turnaround management terms: a bleeder). We don't know the reason for the bleeding but we know we need to act fast and vigilantly. We have two possibilities:

1. Stop the bleeding without looking at the root cause. The bleeding could briefly stop or not, but if we don't fix the cause it will start again and the patient will die.

2. Find the root cause of the bleeding on time, fix what needs to be fixed correctly, and the patient survives and thrives.

You might say the answer is obvious, but it is apparently not so for lots of people. When I arrive at companies that need to be turned around, I see again and again that the same damage has been done by taking the wrong measures to fix the problem, without understanding what the issues really are.

Business owners with no experience of rescuing businesses can't always get it right, but they are also getting bad advice from consultants and interim specialists who think that the only way to save a company is to cut costs. Once the cuts have been made, usually in the wrong places, the interim director leaves, thinking their job is done. In reality, they have just set back the task of rescuing the company; they have destroyed morale and damaged trust in a proper turnaround process.

To successfully turn a business around, we need to stop staring at the bleeding, patch the wound up and speed up the diagnosis of the business. When you know where to look, the diagnosis will take days, not months. This is in contrast to what lots of consulting firms will tell you.

In this chapter I will show you how to look at your business holistically, the key pitfalls to avoid in a turnaround and how I discovered my Fix, Reset and Accelerate method. We will then look at how to apply this method to your business and get it to survive and thrive in twelve months.

Looking holistically at a business

Looking at a business holistically means seeing it as a whole living being. The image above shows this holistic view, which you should refer to as you apply the Fix, Reset and Accelerate process. The key elements of the holistic view are:

1. The **external factors** the business reacts to. What is happening in the economy and the industry will affect it sooner or later. New regulations could change the game; pervasive technological advances can impact the company's market share and competitive position; and new competitors can eat up its market share or in some cases completely replace it.

2. The **external players** that affect it: those who support it, buy from it, fund it, own it, supervise it or have an opinion about it. These external players are the business's lifelines. They need to be kept engaged and on board with the business and its management.

3. The business's **key levers**, which are the tools the leaders use to direct the business towards a successful future, inform and lead their teams, monitor progress, and tell the business how to act and behave.

4. The **core processes** used to manage the business and bring in expertise and to develop, sell, deliver and manage products and services.

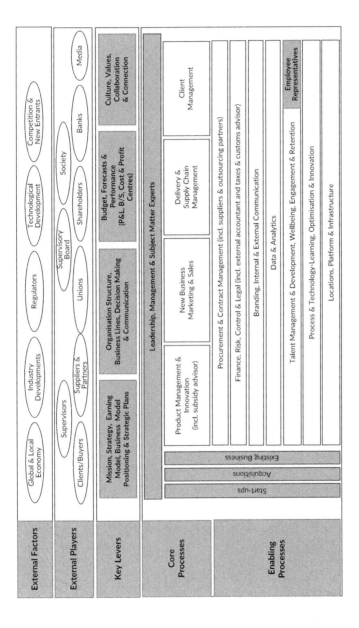

The holistic view of a business

5. The **enabling processes** used to:

   – Find the right suppliers and outsourcing partners, buy from them and manage the contracts with them and their delivery.

   – Manage the financial aspects of the business (order to cash, procure to pay, travel and expenses, record and report) and provide the management with the required data and advice to control the business financials.

   – Communicate internally and externally and increase brand likeability to increase sales and keep employees loyal.

   – Provide the information needed by the business to manage processes, report on them and inform key players about their performance.

   – Manage the business's talent (from quantity and quality standpoints), develop them, take care of their wellbeing and engagement and keep them on board.

   – Facilitate process and technology learning, optimisation and innovation.

   – Provide the work locations needed and an ICT infrastructure to support the business and its development.

Look in particular at how the core and enabling processes have been organised for the existing business, the start-ups and the acquired businesses. The last two (new) parts of the business frequently get forgotten and don't get any support from the enabling processes, which leads them to fail.

When we view the organisation from this holistic perspective, we question the added value of roles and functions. We start asking the right questions about upskilling people and about meeting needs inhouse versus outsourcing. It is useful to remind people when using this model that we don't own departments; we add value to the business. If a department is not adding value in the supply chain, it is burning money. This way of thinking will help you stop turf protection and create a fluid business. To achieve that, you will need servant leadership – leaders who are not thinking about their turf but focusing on the interests of the business, their clients and their people.

Key pitfalls to avoid

When the market shifts and businesses are impacted, most leaders will decide to wait until things go back to normal. They drive down their costs and capacity and wait for better times. The most talented employees notice that their leaders have chosen the wrong strategy, decide not to support it and leave the company. This does reduce costs in the short term but in the long term it damages the business because the people you see leaving at this point are the key talents, the subject matter experts and the go-getters – the people who get things done.

New gaps will then surface because of the loss of these talents and the company will become less able to sell, deliver and manage effectively, efficiently and correctly. Project deadlines and clients' KPIs (key performance indicators) get missed, clients leave and deals are lost to competitors (who now employ the business's former top employees). Clients start paying later or putting invoices on litigation, cash becomes a key concern and profitability starts to fall.

This is the point where the leaders realise they need help. Usually they will bring in a restructuring firm or interim director who will promise to help them improve their profit by driving down costs as fast as possible. This strategy is likely to include eliminating investments to improve the bottom line.

This is a bad prescription for the patient: too little, too late and then the wrong medicine. The chances of a quick recovery and a healthy future will be shrinking by the day. The consequences of focus on survival, with zero plan for the future and not keeping key talent, will damage the business's quality of service in the future. Operational, client, compliance and employee issues will pile up. The cost reductions, which have been made without holistically understanding the impact on the business, will lead to more costs. Not investing (wisely) implies losing market share. This is a narrow-minded, limbic-brain approach to company rescue: a cost-based strategy that is not sustainable.

How I discovered the Fix, Reset and Accelerate method

I had a client who acquired a top-performing financial services advisory company (a medium enterprise). A year or so after the acquisition, regulations changed and with them the market. The entrepreneur started to run down costs to keep the business profitable. This went on over a few years as revenues kept declining. Employees were demotivated and the top performers left. Technological innovation stopped and the company was lagging behind its competitors.

I was called in by the shareholder, who was extremely frustrated with this business and by its 'annoying and frustrating management and employees'. At this point profitability had been declining for years, the business was making losses and could not be sold; it was a money drain.

After a short briefing from the shareholder, I met the management team. After a few hours, I could see opportunities and I knew that they could still make it.

It was worth a try. As they were making losses, I agreed with the management team that I would limit my hours. I would mentor them and they would do the work. Our goal would be to fix and grow the business in twelve months.

We started by developing a targeted performance monitoring that would be used to manage the business and inform the shareholder. We were able to share that information with the shareholder every week. She agreed to step aside and give us space and time to fix the profitability.

We got together with HR and the management team to own the cost, the revenues and outcomes of the interventions, and drive the profitability of the business. They did this by increasing production and thereby revenue, eliminating unnecessary costs and then, later, changing the positioning, pricing and product mix. We invested in technology from the incoming additional revenues and broke even in six months. We ended the year with a great profit, for the first time in years. The management team and their people were thrilled.

They were now trained to run the business and keep it profitable and they showed positive results every month. The shareholder agreed to keep the management team in the lead for managing the business.

Why Fix, Reset and Accelerate worked

We did not hire consultants with major clients, nice written testimonials and big names. We did not have lavish presentations with great graphics, stories and benchmarks.

We did not have young and eager quants (quantitative researchers) with zero business (and business rescue) experience running around talking to employees and making nice graphs. The analysis did not take three months or cost us a fortune.

We agreed the terms and process and started the turnaround in a few days. We worked closely with the management team and HR. We did the full business diagnosis and set up the monitoring in two weeks. In the same two weeks we changed how the management was working as a team, defined solutions for the business, and set up a roadmap and a storyline. We shared and talked about the plans with all employees, got feedback and started the empowerment journey as a team.

From this point, I – together with HR – mentored the management team for a few hours a week; we discussed performance based on monitoring and discussed the execution of the agreed plan. We offered the team, alongside this, a targeted development programme to build their capabilities.

Result: low-cost intervention, more ownership, leadership development, faster outcomes and results that were not only stunning but sustainable.

We achieved these sustainable results with the business's own team; we developed, leveraged and maintained the key talents, built our own hero army and started winning in the market. The employees owned the business and performed as they never had before. The shareholder, watching from the wings, was thrilled. This is how the Fix, Reset and Accelerate model emerged.

It helped that I came to this business with experience as a strategy consultant and had also been a client of a big strategy firm. I had seen the process from both sides at close quarters. I moved on to become a transformation director, then managing director and CEO of a group of companies, always in the transformation and business rescue area. All this helped me understand what works for business rescue and transformation and what doesn't.

If your company needs rescuing, it's best to work with people who have managed business rescue of companies several times – people who can teach your team how to do it and mentor them. The fixing stage needs to start fast (within the first two weeks) and be sustainable; there is no time for trial and error.

You don't need three months for analysis before you start turning around a business. You can start in two weeks, if you know what you should be looking for. You need your own hero army, who know your business, who will grow and stay with you. You don't need big structures, thinktanks and steering committees. Your existing management team needs to do the work of rescuing the business with their people. That should be the top priority item on their agenda.

How to Fix, Reset and Accelerate in twelve months

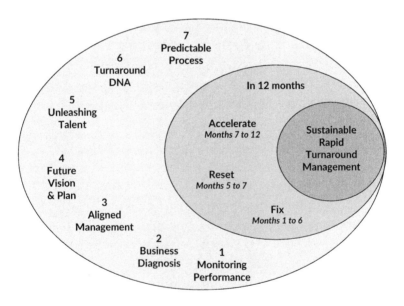

The Fix, Reset, Accelerate model

This process demands speed combined with vigilance. Every move counts and needs to bring you closer to financial stability and profitability, then to a position where you can thrive in your market. The Fix, Reset and Accelerate approach is based on three phases and comprises seven key building blocks, discussed in full in the following chapters:

Building block 1: Monitoring performance (Chapter 5)

From day one you need to increase accountability, transparency and ownership. This starts with pushing down the Profit and Loss Statement and budgets/ forecasts deeper into the organisation to reach profit and cost centres and every individual department and employee. Share the financials with everyone.

From week one, set up a process to monitor the performance of all activities of the business (core processes and enabling processes). Identify crisp indicators: a few factors that make or break the performance in each area. This will help you to improve fast. You get what you measure.

Building block 2: Business diagnosis (Chapter 6)

This is the process of finding out how the business is really doing and what is going wrong from a holistic point of view, and understanding the root causes and the impact in the short and long term. You need to understand the symptoms to find out what caused the illness. When you fix the root cause and remove the impact, the symptoms should disappear.

Building block 3: Aligned management (Chapter 7)

To Fix, Reset and Accelerate a business, it is crucial that the management team is fully on board with the turnaround approach, the profitability improvement measures to be taken, the chosen strategy, business model, earning model and how the company is being led during the three phases of the turnaround.

Any lack of alignment will be obvious in the organisation. On day one of this programme, look closely at the quality of your management team and the alignment of their perception and thinking. You can't steer a ship through a storm with a quarrelling crew; delaying these decisions will have disastrous effects.

Building block 4: Future vision and plan (Chapter 8)

A vision inspires people. The conviction that you can collectively make it happen connects the team and unleashes the energy the leaders, their teams and employees need.

Your vision is fundamental in guiding the direction of your business, helping to define short- and long-term goals and providing the framework for decisions.

Next to your vision, you will need a plan. The plan for the Fix, Reset and Accelerate is iterative in nature; the knowledge you acquire from each phase will inspire the plan of the next one. You draw your roadmap for the twelve months after you have done your business diagnosis and worked out solutions with your management team. In week one you will plan the Fix phase in detail and start carrying it out. In the first week of month five, you will repeat this process for the Reset phase. In the first week of month seven, based on the outcomes of the Fix and Reset phase, you will plan the Accelerate phase.

Building block 5: Unleashing talent (Chapter 9)

There is so much talent left untapped in most organisations. Scouting talent, allocating people to projects that match their talent and giving them proper and relevant education will help you build your entire Fix, Reset and Accelerate hero army in around six months, which will help accelerate the transformation of your business.

If done in a targeted way, this development should not cost a lot. The people that you upskill and right-skill will be contributing to your programme at an early stage and will be the next leaders of your business.

Investing in your people will increase loyalty and quality of outcomes (in operations and projects) and will save you money on hiring for leadership roles in the (near) future.

How many people do you need in your hero army? Around 15% of your people is reasonable, evenly distributed over all departments and organisational levels (directors, managers and employees). They should be the most talented, qualified and respected people in their teams. They will become the energy starters through your whole company and the ones who will bring others along. When you can't find a candidate for your hero army in a department, fix that gap. That's an urgent quality problem.

Building block 6: Turnaround DNA (Chapter 10)

Once you have selected your top 15%, they need to start learning the skills for the turnaround and transformation of businesses. These skills will directly help them to effectively contribute to improving profitability, resetting the strategy, positioning, earning and business models and thereby moving your business faster than the competition towards the conditions that will make it thrive.

When I work with clients, I take their hero army through the Turnaround and Transformation Academy I developed with my team to acquire the skills that will make them transformational leaders. Having these skills embedded in your top 15% will energise the organisation, create a common language and align people from all departments around the transformation goals of the Fix, Reset and Accelerate programme.

Building block 7: Predictable process (Chapter 11)

You need to discuss with your team how you are going to run this major business turnaround and how you are going to inform your organisation and relevant key external players.

Are you going to work in projects? Who is leading the projects? Who is owning them? Who will be involved? Where and when are decisions going to be taken? When and where will employee representatives be involved or asked to approve decisions? How are you going to inform the company about your plans? When and how are you going to inform external players?

A transparent and clear process, with people informed and able to interact and ask questions, inspires trust and increases engagement in the organisation, leaving no room for toxicity and politics. Transparency and clarity are keys to the success of this programme.

I will share how I structure my programmes, using a simple step-by-step model. This model will help you simplify your Fix, Reset and Accelerate programme, manage the involvement of your stakeholders, keep monitoring the profitability and performance of the business, ensure timely decision-making with your management team and manage the big changes that need to happen and the flow of communication. You will be able to keep on top of the turnaround phases, their deliverables and how employees are feeling during the whole process.

What happens in the three phases

Phase 1: Fix (months 1 to 6)

The focus in this phase is on fixing your performance holistically and building your hero army. To do this, as outlined earlier, you need to set up holistic monitoring of the business and do an in-depth diagnosis to understand what is going wrong and define the root causes of the problem. The holistic model of the business presented earlier in this chapter will help you in this step. Get your management team in place, keep it as small as you can and make sure the whole team is aligned around how to solve the issues you have identified, with each of them owning the profit and loss of their profit and/or cost centre.

Your focus will be on getting the business functioning properly, fixing the root causes, improving performance and making the business profitable again in six months. One of the causes will be the organisational pathologies caused by the crisis, as discussed in Chapter 2.

Don't get lost in strategy discussions but be clear about the identity and ambition of your company and affirm your belief that you will achieve that ambition. You need that positive energy to keep the company going.

In this phase you will scout the talent needed to build your hero army, start training them and get them involved in this programme. Use non-disclosure agreements (NDAs) and point out why trust is key, as they will have access to confidential information before the rest of the organisation.

Phase 2: Reset (months 5 to 7)

In this phase you will be defining your strategy, earning model and business model, and developing a plan for future-proofing your business.

After five months in the Fix phase, having taken the right steps to fix your performance and profitability, you will be moving towards your break-even point and seeing the financials improving steadily every month. This is the time to start thinking about strategy, earning model and business model, and developing a plan for transforming your business. In this step you need to take into consideration the impact of the Fourth Industrial Revolution, the UN's

Sustainable Global Goals and the Great Reset (discussed in Chapter 1) on the future of your company and include them in your plan to make your business thrive.

Refer to the holistic model earlier in this chapter to translate strategy into execution. With your hero army, think through what needs to change in your products and services, core processes and enabling processes.

Maintain those monitoring processes you set up in the Fix phase and introduce additional metrics to monitor the business after the planned changes. Use the holistic model to translate the changes into every process and thereby every fibre of your organisation.

The Reset period is the time to reaffirm the alignment of the management team and improve your team dynamics. Make detailed execution plans, allocate project leads and owners, and agree the processes for governance, decision-making and communication, and required consultation with employee representatives. Inform the entire organisation about the plans, get feedback and engagement, and work out how to keep people informed.

The hero army will complete their training during this phase; you can put them in charge of your strategic transformation projects.

Phase 3: Accelerate (months 7 to 12)

This is where you build and execute the plans for the Accelerate phase with your newly developed hero army and start increasing your profitability and market share.

Use the holistic model to monitor the changes. Keep the management aligned. With your hero army in charge of projects, build your Accelerate phase plan in week one, and start the roll-out in a structured way to align your earning model and business model to your updated strategy and move your organisation to a place from which it can thrive.

It is essential to keep monitoring your business and to manage projects and decision-making closely. Keep a watch on (project) dependencies and increase collaboration between teams.

The transition from the old business model to the new needs to run smoothly to avoid impacting profitability. This means taking a risk-averse approach by making changes incrementally. Keep communication and required consultations with employee representatives flowing and keep the entire organisation in the know. Encourage feedback and engagement.

Summary

A sustainable turnaround of a business demands speed combined with vigilance. It is essential to look holistically at your business when preparing for a turnaround and to focus on sustainable outcomes instead of a quick fix. Every move counts and needs to bring you closer to financial stability and profitability, then to a position where you can thrive in your market.

I introduced you in this chapter to the three steps you need to take for achieving this sustainable turnaround – Fix, Reset and Accelerate – and outlined its seven building blocks. I will now move on to introduce you to the building blocks in more detail, starting in the next chapter where we will look closely at effective tools and methods to monitor the performance of your business.

5
Building Block 1 – Monitoring Performance

Whenever you go into a company that has (financially) hit the wall and start asking questions to get a holistic view of the company's health and performance, two things happen: you get incomplete and incorrect answers, and you get them too late. Always start with monitoring performance to understand and improve your business. A severely ill and bleeding patient needs to be attached to a monitor so you can observe their vital functions and decide when and how to intervene.

When the monitoring is as holistic as possible and it is happening frequently enough or, even better, in real time, you will receive important insights into what is going wrong and where, the pace of recovery as the business responds to your interventions and what is needed to improve its long-term health and stamina.

To monitor the health and performance of your business during and after the Fix, Reset and Accelerate programme, you need to know:

- What you need to monitor, when and why

- How to deal with obstacles as you put monitoring in place

- What to do with your monitoring information once you get it

- How to use the monitoring information to mobilise your organisation

What, when and why to monitor

You need monitoring from day one to increase awareness, transparency, accountability and ownership in your management team and in the organisation as a whole.

Your management team and employees need to be shown how the business is doing, and how their actions and contributions impact the business. They can then understand what they need to do more and less of to help the business survive and thrive. Remember that employees and management are invested in the business. They have chosen to work for this business and they need it to make a living. If they are involved, treated decently, cared for, appreciated and not lied to, they will do whatever it takes to save the business and help it thrive.

To bring the financial results of the business closer to the people in it, you will need to translate your totalised P&L (profit and loss – actuals, budgets and reforecasts) into sub-P&Ls for your profit centres and cost centres. I will tell you how to do this shortly.

You will need also to define the key drivers (KPIs) for all functions in your business – what it is that generates value by directly or indirectly leading to an increase in revenue generation or increase in productivity. As an example, without HR hiring talent there will be no delivery of products and services to clients. Delivery of products and services increases revenue generation. Talent management therefore indirectly drives revenue generation.

When you start working on monitoring, you will find that only a few members of your management team, if any, are already monitoring their own KPIs. Start with the level of monitoring that the management team can deliver and keep pushing for more, until you can oversee the health and performance of the whole business. The more monitoring you start pulling, the more issues will start surfacing, the more ownership you will get and the more traction and speed you will generate for solving the issues of business.

A few years ago I started working on the rescue of a business on the twentieth of the month. After the end of the financial month, I had a meeting with the management team. I asked the financial director to present the financials; his answer was that they were not available for another fifteen days. This meant that the business was flying blind for forty-five days.

I turned to the operations director and asked how we had performed in terms of delivery to clients and revenue generation. The operations director did not know. Financials needed to come from finance. No KPIs were available. So it went on. The commercial director had no client performance data. The support departments did not know whether their spend was on budget and had no KPIs to track value generation. They were all waiting to be told by finance, fifteen days after the month closing, whether they were hitting budget. This is common practice in lots of businesses. I told the management team that they were not in control operationally or financially and that this would need to change from that day. The only way to turn the business around was to get in control. They needed to start proactively managing instead of being forty-five days late.

Distribute the P&L

Start by transferring the ownership of parts of the P&L to the functional areas of the business. The CEO and CFO should not be the only people worrying about the financial outcomes; performance is everybody's job. Ownership of the P&L should come with the management team t-shirt. Every management team member should translate the P&L to their direct reports and to all employees in their functional area, to increase awareness, transparency, accountability and ownership – and, above all, pride. How awesome would it be if you knew that by overperforming this month your department had moved the needle from loss to profit, and that you would be praised for that in a town hall meeting? You would know that you and your team were making a difference to the business and you would want to do it again.

The graphic below shows how you can distribute the P&L. Here are some examples:

- Your sales director is responsible for the recurring and non-recurring revenues, for their number of FTEs (Full Time Equivalent of an employee workweek), and for their FTE-related and non-FTE-related indirect cost. It is key that she/he manages to increase the recurring revenues.

Total Profit & Loss Statement

Total Profit & Loss Statement	Budget FTEs	Actual FTEs	Budget Performance	Actuals Performance	Sales	Delivery	R&D	Marketing & Branding	Technology & Change	HR	Finance Risk & Facilities
Total Recurring Revenues					Owner	Owner					
Total Non Recurring Revenues					Owner						
Total Revenues					Owner	Owner					
KPI: % Increase in Recurring revenues					Owner						
Total Number of Direct FTEs	FTEs	FTEs				Owner					
FTE Related Recurring Direct Cost	FTEs	FTEs				Owner					
FTE Related Non Recurring Direct Cost	FTEs	FTEs				Owner					
Non-FTE Related Recurring Direct Cost						Owner					
Non-FTE Related Non Recurring Direct Cost						Owner					
Total Direct Cost						Owner					
KPIs % Increase in Productivity (Direct Cost)						Owner					
Recurring Gross Margin											
Non Recurring Gross Margin											
Total Gross Margin											
Total Number of Indirect FTEs	FTEs	FTEs									
FTE Related Indirect Cost	FTEs										
R&D	FTEs						Owner				
Client Management	FTEs				Owner						
Sales – New business	FTEs				Owner						
Marketing & Branding	FTEs							Owner			
Technology	FTEs								Owner		
Change	FTEs								Owner		
HR	FTEs									Owner	
Finance Risk & Compliance	FTEs										Owner
Facilities	FTEs										Owner

Non-FTE Related Indirect Cost									
R&D									
Client Management				Owner					
Sales – New business	Owner								
Marketing & Branding	Owner								
Technology		Owner							
Change		Owner							
HR			Owner						
Finance Risk & Compliance					Owner				
Facilities					Owner				
Building					Owner				
Utilities					Owner				
Other (Non-FTE) Operating Expenses					Owner				
Recurring Indirect Cost									
Non Recurring Indirect Cost									
Total Indirect Cost									
KPIs % increase in Productivity (Indirect Cost)	Owner	Owner	Owner	Owner	Owner				
Total Recurring Expenses									
Total Non Recurring Expenses									
Total Operating Expenses									
Recurring EBITDA									
Non Recurring EBITDA									
EBITDA									
Depreciation & Amortisation									
Interest									
Recurring Earning BT									
Non Recurring Earning BT									
Earnings Before Tax									
Taxes									
Recurring Net Profit									
Non Recurring Net Profit									
Net Profit									

Profit & Loss Statement

- Your delivery director is responsible for the recurring revenues generated through the delivery of products and services, for their FTEs and for the recurring and non-recurring FTE-related and non-FTE-related cost. It is key that she/he manages to increase the recurring revenues and improve productivity.

The rest of the redistribution is less complex; enabling functions are responsible for staying within budget in terms of number of FTEs, FTE-related indirect cost and non-FTE-related indirect cost.

Make it a priority for your finance director and team to work on this and align where needed with the functional heads. If finance is in control, they will have already defined profit centres and cost centres in the financial system. They will need to work with HR to link FTE data to the P&L and with the management team members to understand what is recurring and non-recurring revenue and spend, if they don't know already.

You need a tech-savvy person in your finance department to turn this overview into an automatically generated monthly report. If that person is not there, start thinking about hiring one or pulling someone in from another department.

The previous graphic shows how to redistribute your P&L.

A few days of working on this will show you where your business is going wrong financially. You will be able to point out the areas which need to do better. The discussion will shift from 'we did not do well last month and we need to understand why' to 'please tell me why you did not hit your budget'. Once you make this shift, people will start analysing their P&L before coming to the meeting. They will start tracking their FTEs and costs in their department instead of waiting for finance to come up with the numbers. That is ownership.

You can translate this information into graphs, comparing performance to budget in total and per department, and share it in town hall meetings, getting everybody to own the financial performance. Once ownership has been widely spread, the effect is amazing. Teams will start thinking proactively to improve their financial results.

Key performance indicators (KPIs)

Now that we have the management team and employees to look after the revenue generation and managing cost, let's look at the key drivers that influence profitability.

There are two ways to generate money within your (and every) business:

1. Increase revenue generation by enhancing customer value (making customers spend more with you instead of with competitors) and finding new revenue opportunities

2. Increase productivity by improving cost structure and increasing the utilisation of assets

Plotting this on the core processes and enabling processes of the organisation, which I introduced in the holistic model in the previous chapter, will help us define the key KPIs we need to manage the business.

The following table shows the KPIs for the various functional areas that I always begin with. Start with these and evolve from there.

Value	KPIs
Sales	Growth in revenues
Increase revenue generation	Existing and new clients
	Existing and new business
	Speed and quality of request resolution
	Speed and quality of complaint resolution
	Timely payment of invoices by clients
Increase productivity	Productivity of own team

Value	KPIs
Delivery	Delivery as per budget
Increase revenue generation	Timely payment of invoices by clients
	Improve quality
	Improve customer satisfaction
	Improve customer retention
	Speed and quality of request resolution
	Speed and quality of complaint resolution
	Customer repeated sales
	Increased customer spend
Increase productivity	Improvement in productivity
Research and development (R&D)	Profitability of products and services
	Time to market
Increase revenue generation	Customer satisfaction with new products and services
	ROI (return on investment) R&D
	Progress reporting development (progress and budget conformance)
	Budget and time conformance
Increase productivity	Improvement in productivity

Value	KPIs
Marketing and branding	Increased brand awareness
	Increased brand preference
Increase revenue generation	Increased sales conversion
	Increased sales
	Speed and quality of online complaint/ exposure resolution
Increase productivity	Improvement in productivity
Technology and change	Time to market of changes
	(Speed and quality of) issue resolutions
Increase revenue generation	Business satisfaction (R&D, delivery, sales and enabling functions)
	Progress reporting projects (progress and budget conformance)
Increase productivity	Improvement in productivity and efficiency
	Budget and time conformance of projects and changes
Talent management and development (HR)	Quality and quantity of talent
	Retention
	Development
	Health and wellbeing
Increase revenue generation	Recruitment
	Satisfaction and engagement
Increase productivity	Improvement in productivity

Value	KPIs
Finance, risk and facilities Increase revenue generation	Faster (financial month) closing Business controlling quality and risk management P&L monitoring • Management of spend (procurement). • Management of FTE spend. • Conformance to budget and reforecast (overall). • Quality of support in facilities. Balance sheet management • Cash conversion (management of inventory/work in progress and collection of accounts receivable). Yearly improvement. Compare over five to ten years. • Fixed asset turnover (efficiency of asset utilisation to generate revenue). Yearly improvement. Compare over five to ten years. • Return on assets (efficiency of asset utilisation to generate profit/net income). Yearly improvement. Compare over five to ten years.
Increase productivity	Improvement in productivity

Where you can improve your profit margin

Besides making the management team and their teams own their section of the company P&L and managing them on the key drivers that generate value, we need to address areas that will improve your profit margin.

Employee satisfaction, engagement, health and wellbeing

The quality of the internal organisation and how people are led determines the quality of service and tone of voice towards the customer, which translates into customer satisfaction, which translates into loyalty, which leads to increased customer spend and increased revenues. Happy customers bring more happy customers.

Track employee satisfaction, employee engagement, and health and wellbeing to ensure that your employees are happy. Improve the quality of the internal organisation (management and communication, goal-setting, processes, procedures, system quality, development, growth and reward) and see employee and customer satisfaction increase.

Happy people produce quality and increase profit.

Timeliness and completeness of client invoicing

Ensure that work in progress ('inventory' in your balance sheet) is delivered to clients faster and that it is translated into invoicing as per agreed payment schedules.

Check how clients are paying invoices ('accounts receivable' in your balance sheet). When you find delays (in 'days outstanding'), track customer satisfaction and the quality of complaint and request resolution. Get your delivery and sales teams to solve these issues and you will get cash in faster.

Use client contracts to understand whether you are charging everything you need to charge or missing any revenues. Check whether you are applying a proper indexation of your prices and follow up on agreed price increases.

Procurement, external spend and suppliers

Centralise the management of procurement and spend. Ensure that the management and employees understand you are doing this to review contracts and improve margins.

Ensure also that you can take the required decisions for your team quickly and that you are not slowing down your business. Tighten procurement controls – ask: 'Do we really need this?' Check payments and challenge invoices.

Use your supplier contracts to understand whether you are being charged too much, get refunds where relevant and end contracts for things your business no longer needs. Renegotiate existing contracts and change suppliers to cut costs and improve quality and delivery.

Remove underperformance

Look at the cost of underperformance in the processes in your company. When an employee is making lots of mistakes because they are not fit for the job, they cause more work for others, create dissatisfied colleagues and customers and damage your brand loyalty. Unfit employees need to be dealt with early in this process in an honourable way, in conjunction with HR and the relevant manager.

Manage your R&D and project spend

Stop spending on innovation until you are in control of your project portfolio. Analyse your portfolio in the first week so as not to disadvantage vital projects. Challenge the value projects are adding in terms of revenue generation and productivity, check how they conform to your plan and budget, and check the quality of the project management and project team.

Only continue with projects that really add value to the business. Change the project managers and team members of these key projects if the current ones are not delivering (while burning your R&D, change and innovation budget).

Manage the profitability of products/ services and clients

Track the profitability of products and services and of client contracts to understand what is making money and what is not. Can you scale up a product/service? Sell it to more clients? Increase productivity and thereby generate more margin? If products are not making money, renegotiate contracts with clients or eliminate what is not profitable. This will be a tough concept for your team to swallow. Share the numbers, discuss, find solutions collectively and act quickly but vigilantly. Remind your team that a product/ service or client that is not making money is eating up profitability. That needs to change.

Balance your overheads

Track and monitor your overhead/delivery ratio. Traditionally you needed to have a maximum of 25% overhead vs 75% delivery FTEs. Now we need to take into account digital, AI and robotics and their impact on productivity in delivery.

Protect your brand

Monitor your social media and prevent bad comments from damaging your sales and revenue. Make somebody responsible for monitoring this and responding to comments within an hour. Coordinate with delivery and enabling functions for speedy resolution of issues and complaints.

Increase your asset utilisation

Check with your finance director and team:

- How much revenue is generated by your company's total assets (this can be done by checking your fixed asset turnover).

- How well your company is using its assets to generate profit. This can be done by calculating your return on assets ratio.

Compare these to competitors – your competitors' Profit and Loss Statement (P&L) and Balance Sheet (B/S) are public information and can be requested from the local chamber of commerce. This will help you understand how you are performing in the eyes of your shareholders.

If you tighten the investment decisions and the management of R&D, innovation and change projects, these metrics will start improving over time.

How to deal with monitoring-related obstacles

Readily available and good-quality data is crucial for moving towards more control and predictability of outcomes, which is pivotal for your turnaround programme. You will need a top-notch analytics person as you Fix, Reset and Accelerate. If you don't have one, solve that fast.

Data quality improvement will need to become a core element of your programme. You can't manage a business with erroneous data. Fix it.

If finance becomes a bottleneck for delivering data, decentralise first to collect data and consolidate with finance later. Every department leader needs to start managing their part of the business and clarifying why things are underperforming or improving. Do not allow your people to point fingers at IT and finance: get them support on analytics, give them raw data and let them make an effort to understand their performance and define their KPI reports. Challenge the data with your finance director. Push for teamwork and collaboration.

What to do with your data

From week one, ask the management team to start reporting on their KPIs and set up one-to-one meetings. They should already have access to the information they need in their systems. Don't ask for fancy automated reports – Excel sheets or screen dumps will do at the beginning. As long as they are digging into their own information systems, talking to their managers and employees and understanding what is happening, you are making progress. The improvement process has begun. Keep pushing until reliable reporting is formalised.

If you push for improvement in the defined KPIs and for conformance to budget and reforecasts, you will start seeing your performance improve.

How to use monitoring to mobilise your organisation

Share monthly reports on financial performance and KPI performance with all employees. Share successes and challenges. Give your managers and their teams credit for the improvements in their area and let them share their successes in town hall meetings. Engage in dialogue with employees. Get everybody involved in the improvement of the performance and KPIs. Nominate winning teams and give prizes.

Summary

A strong beginning to the Fix, Reset and Accelerate programme is the set-up of a monitoring system for your business that will help you monitor your business's health and performance through the process, and afterwards. I told you when and what you need to monitor and why; how to deal with the obstacles that stand in your way for getting the monitoring in place; what you should do with the monitoring information once you get it; and how to use the monitoring to mobilise your organisation.

Next, we look at how to perform a proper diagnosis of your business.

6
Building Block 2 – Business Diagnosis

The first questions from shareholders or business owners during a turnaround are always about what is going wrong and the best way to save the company and go back to profit and growth.

Let's return for a moment to the parallel with the sick and bleeding patient. A thorough and speedy diagnosis is needed to understand what really caused the bleeding, so that when we fix the root cause the patient starts to make a sustainable recovery and is eventually able to not only survive but thrive.

I diagnose by asking questions, collecting data, plotting that information on my holistic company model to gain a helicopter view of the business and performing a root cause analysis. The first time I did a turnaround, the large number of issues in the company seemed overwhelming and I did not know where to start. But over time I saw a pattern across each company I worked with and developed a set of focused questions and models that still help me achieve a high-speed diagnosis.

In this chapter I will tell you:

- What to look for in companies that hit the wall

- The questions to ask and the data to collect for an effective diagnosis

- How you can plot the issues you discover to get a helicopter view of the business

- How to perform a root cause analysis and use the results to engage your management team and employees in problem-solving, as well as keeping your stakeholders informed

What happens when companies hit the wall

A company crisis usually starts with something happening externally that reduces its earning capacity. The company is then still in its comfort zone (a state of inertia). It does not realise that the game has changed and does not react adequately or quickly enough.

The consequences, in short, are top-line issues: costs becoming too high, profitability decreasing, or stress in the leadership and management layer which translates into issues in the workforce. The company then tries to fix the profitability problem, usually by cutting costs and jobs. Organisational pathologies develop, talent starts leaving the company, quality and overall performance deteriorate, and change and innovation projects get delayed. Client satisfaction drops and so, soon after, does client retention and profitability.

By this point the stakeholders are worried (including clients, suppliers, employee representatives, shareholders, banks, market supervisors) and the company goes into a death spiral.

Questions to ask and data and information to collect

When I start a turnaround project, I ask the shareholders or owners of the business to tell me what they think is going on. Before starting the programme I will also try to meet the management team and key stakeholders and ask them the same question. Everybody looks at the business from their own perspective and will tell you what they are particularly worried about. When you gather all that information and add the financial information and metrics of the business, a diagnosis becomes easier.

In mid-crisis you will hear lots of subjective perspectives, which reflect the organisational pathologies going on in the business. The facts and financials will help you decide later which version is right.

Here is what I include in my standard facts and financials request:

1. The strategy and business plan of the business (for this year and last).

2. The commercial pitch of the business for clients and partners (what are you telling the market?).

3. The financials budget and year to date (YTD) actuals P&L and B/S totalised, and for each profit centre and cost centre. For the P&L, a detailed overview of the past five years of all items from the financial system.

4. Log of the meetings with the shareholders for the past three months.

5. Current governance and decision-making structure.

6. A high-level and detailed organisation chart of the business, showing distribution of employees and the development and number of employees over the past three years (from HR).

7. End of year review of the management and employees and salary raises (and bonuses).

8. Report of the last employee satisfaction/engagement survey and overviews of sickness rates, attrition and recruiting.

9. Reports of meetings with the employee representatives over the past three months.

10. Results of the last customer satisfaction survey and a report of client requests and complaints resolution.

11. Recent reports about profitability of products and services and client contracts.

12. The sales pipeline.

13. Delivery dashboard (for tracking delivery and client KPIs).

14. Log of client issues and complaints.

15. Log of meetings with the market supervisor over the past three months.

16. Project portfolio overview, budget and YTD financials of projects; and project progress reports (goals, progress, status, budget and YTD financials for each project).

17. Accounts receivable/days outstanding report from finance.

18. Procedure for external spend and overview of contracts.

19. Available information about the performance of marketing, communication and branding.

20. Download of the company dashboard that the management team is using for steering the business.

I have not yet visited a company where the management team could deliver even one-third of this information. Don't worry, it isn't the end of the world. This is an indication of the areas where you have more work to do. The fact that the management team members will have to tell you that they don't have that information will make them understand what is not being managed and you will start seeing action on those items.

Alongside the information you are gathering, use the holistic model of the business that we discussed in Chapter 4 to gain insight into all areas of the business.

Plotting the issues on the holistic model

Based on your interviews with the shareholders, management team and key stakeholders, and the documents you receive, you will begin putting red flags in the areas with issues.

When the turnaround has been started too late, wrong interventions have been performed and the business is already making losses, there will be red flags

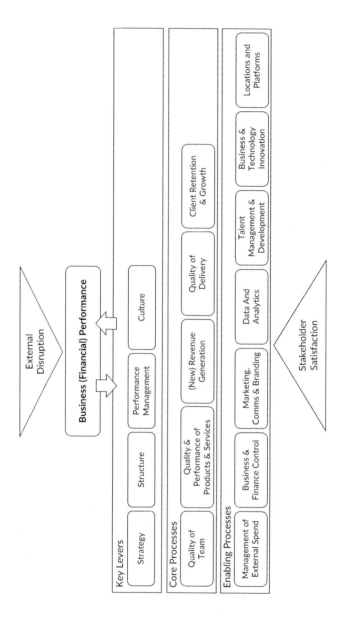

Plotting the issues

everywhere, meaning lots of fixing to do. It is tempting to start running towards solutions, but your first step should be to slow down and find the root causes. Going slow at this point means you will pick up speed later on the right issues.

How to perform a root cause analysis

When I do a root cause analysis (also called a cause and effect analysis), I use a Japanese model called the Ishikawa (or fishbone diagram).[20] It is a Lean Six Sigma model used during process optimisation for finding potential causes of a specific event. It works well at process level and it also can work at organisational level during turnaround programmes to find reasons for declining profitability.

Below is a generic fishbone model customised for turnarounds.

This is how you use the fishbone model to find root causes:

1. Determine the problem statement and write it at the right side of the model; the head of the fishbone. In turnarounds the issue is evident: there is an issue with the (financial) performance. You can then specify what exactly is happening in

---

20   Originally devised by Kaoru Ishikawa, the Japanese organisational theorist.

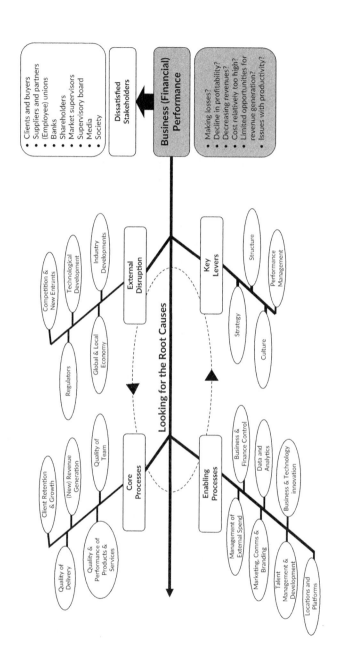

Root cause analysis for turnarounds

the business. Losses? Decline in profitability? Decreasing revenues? Cost too high? Limited opportunities for revenue generation? Issues with productivity?

2. Define which stakeholders are dissatisfied with the performance of the business. Highlight them in this list: clients and buyers, suppliers and partners, (employee) unions, banks, shareholders, market supervisors, the supervisory board, the media, the general public. You will need to start involving these stakeholders and informing them about your findings and your process.

3. Highlight, based on your findings from meetings and the reports and documents you receive, the categories from the holistic model list (external disruption, key levers, enabling processes and core processes) where you find issues.

4. Now go a step further to identify sub-causes attached to the branches (or fine bones) of each category cause.

The outcome will look like this:

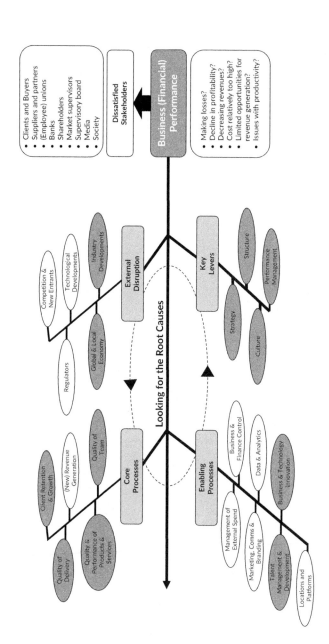

A completed root cause analysis diagram

Once you highlight the issues, you will reach a coherent view of what is happening in the business and you can build your storyline towards your management team, employees and relevant stakeholders. Using this model in your discussions with your management team will help everyone to understand what is causing which issue, as the issues are impacting each other.

For instance, a recruiter in HR left the company. Because of that employees were not hired on time and now the business is not delivering within budget. A few hours spent with the management team going through this model in detail delivers great insights and a comprehensive list of root causes. Fixing these will make a big impact on your financial performance.

This model will help you explain what is going on to all levels of the organisation, from production employees to shareholders, and help you engage people in finding solutions. You can also use it to track progress by turning items 'green' when they are achieved. This will help you demonstrate the progress you and your management team are making to your employees, shareholders and stakeholders.

Summary

Learning about business diagnosis will help you understand the general patterns you see in companies that hit the wall, the questions you need to ask, and the data and information you need to collect for the diagnosis. Plotting the issues you discover in a holistic model helps you to gain a helicopter view over the issues of the business, from which point you can perform a root cause analysis and start using that information for engaging your management team and employees in problem-solving, and informing your stakeholders about the issues at hand and how they are being resolved.

7
Building Block 3 – Aligned Management

We all have experienced the power of a great team at least once in our lives. That moment when you feel part of something bigger, when you feel that you belong, that your contribution matters and that you are treated as an equal part of a strong tribe. It is in those moments of cohesion that the whole becomes stronger than the sum of the parts and co-creation emerges. To experience being part of an aligned team and to know that you have each other's backs, that you can help each other to grow, advance and get things done is a magical feeling.

I experienced that feeling when I did my MBA at Nyenrode Business University in the Netherlands. As a study group we had to promise that the whole cohort would make it and that we would help each other succeed. We had two amazing years: working hard, watching over each other, trusting each other, caring for each other with zero ego and having lots of fun. That is how we are supposed to lead in companies to make teams great and make work a pleasure.

Every time I join a company to do transformation or turnaround work, I build a pack. I set up learning opportunities and fun for my team members and see them grow and achieve great collective success. Every time I finish a project, I leave behind a bunch of talented, eager and trustworthy professionals who will develop others and help the company thrive.

Weak teams and sick organisations

Sometimes the team-building task is not so easy. I always come into a business with great plans to create an amazing working environment, heal the organisation, propagate trust, help people grow, fix the business and get it to win in its market, yet I have sometimes been confronted with obstacles as soon as I meet the management team.

In some cases, problems stem from unethical people in leadership positions. They typically have massive egos (think chest-beating silverback gorillas) and strive for power at the expense of others and the business. This leads to a dysfunctional leadership team where there is no trust or culture of taking responsibility and being accountable. Conflicts are avoided or brushed aside and the focus is on survival and guarding turf rather than on results. Lack of trust spreads through the whole organisation. Everybody wants to know everything, decisions are avoided or delayed, decisions that have been made are not respected, and processes are not respected. Plans never move past the planning stage. Suspicion, gossip and rumours are the norm and there seems always to be negative tension. I think of this as a state of organisational neglect.

Once you have worked on the monitoring of the business and its diagnosis, the issues in the company will be exposed and you will create a new culture of accountability, which presents extra stress for the management team. How the team reacts to this will show you how far ego-driven leadership is part of the root cause. Like fish, organisations rot from the head; if you want to fix the organisation fast, that is where you need to start. This will send a clear signal to the organisation that you are serious about change.

When you add dysfunctional behaviour in teams to a company crisis, this becomes a toxic cocktail. Maybe you will be able to steer through the storm with a quarrelling crew but it will be an awful and unpredictable process for yourself as leader and for the rest of the organisation. Solve any issues within your leadership team as early as you can in the turnaround process, before you start if possible. With a healthy team, you will go faster, you will inspire your organisation towards positive change, people will feel safe, grow and learn to trust again. You will have more fun and sustainable results.

No consultants can do this for you. In my experience, the intervention of culture consultants tends to increase dysfunctional behaviour and politics. The silverback gorillas will be the only ones who benefit. You will need to deal with this yourself.

This chapter shows you:

- How to choose your people
- The leadership style that works for organisations that have suffered neglect
- The leadership style you need for turning around businesses

How to choose your people

One of the best books I read early in my career was *How to Become CEO* by Jeffrey J Fox.[21] Fox advised using the three I's – integrity, intelligence and an 'I can do it' attitude – when choosing who to hire, and then over-investing in them (both in salary terms and emotionally, in terms of praise, encouragement and freedom). I have been applying these principles since I started

---

21   JJ Fox, *How to Become CEO: The rules for rising to the top of any organization* (Hachette, 1998)

leading teams and later organisations and have found them to be 100% effective.

People in key (leadership) and influential positions will need the three I's; intelligence will help them fix problems, an 'I can do it' mentality will help them take initiative, and integrity will create fairness, trust and enable teamwork. I learned from turning around businesses that if an 'I' is missing in a management team member, replacement is the best option. This really is a fool-proof recipe if you want to Fix, Reset and Accelerate the business fast and get rid of organisational pathologies.

Next to the three I's, your management team members should be top notch in their functional area, good with their financials, understand IT and be able to run projects. They need also to have good people skills and be transformational leaders.

As you work through the first few months of turn-around – monitoring, diagnosis and fixing projects – you will have intense dialogue with the individual management team members and you will be able to assess them individually. Talking to employee representatives will give you information about the organisation that you won't be getting from your management team.

When combined with the monitoring and diagnosis of the business, you can fairly assess who should stay and who should go. If you decide to let people go, handle the exit in an honourable way. Talk to the individual, keep it professional, open and fair and let them go in a discreet and kind way. Never badmouth them after their exit. This is your chance to set a leadership example.

Leadership for neglected organisations

Neglected organisations are like neglected children. You need to understand this psychological neglect phenomenon, what causes it and how to fix it, and the leadership style that works best in these situations.

Neglect is defined in psychology as deficiency or negligence from a caregiver towards a child. The neglectful caregiver shows lack of empathetic involvement and emotional availability in how they treat the child. The child feels unheard and as if their needs don't matter. If this pattern continues it leads to a growing risk of psychological damage and disrupted development of the child – in other words, trauma.[22] Managers and leaders, as caregivers of a company, can cause the same effect on employees. Both relationships are based on dependency and inequality of power.

---

22 J Kampen, *Emotional Abuse and Neglect in the Workplace* (Palgrave Macmillan, 2015)

A child who has suffered from neglect will develop behavioural problems, whether internalised or externalised; their self-image and self-esteem (defined by being loveable and capable) will be severely damaged. They will start seeing people as unreliable and have difficulties trusting others, developing an insecure attachment style (avoidant, ambivalent or disorganised). The child learns not to call on their parents when they experience stress but will more likely direct their pain, sadness or fear inwards or react aggressively to stress. They are likely to become depressed, anxious or withdrawn, act out towards others (anger, rebellion or aggression) and violate rules. In social contacts they will be distant as they don't trust the inconsistent behaviour of the caregiver from whom they expected nurturing and security. Replace caregiver with employer/manager and child with employee and you will see how this is affecting the business.

Ask for a report from the HR department about sickness rates in neglected organisations and you will see a long duration of sickness ranging from one to twelve months and people relapsing in sickness and burnout cases. Neglect leads to physical and mental health problems (high blood pressure, heart problems, depression, fear and burnout).

When you start working on a turnaround of a business, you have the chance to become the caregiver. You will need a good leadership team on board, consistent leadership behaviour, a targeted development programme and a new style of communicating and interacting with people in the organisation. With these ingredients it will take around six months to help the organisation recover.

To achieve this, employees will need to feel heard and know that their emotions matter. Engage in dialogue with employees; run surveys, ask for feedback and help employees express their unmet needs by the business. You will need to reparent them and rebuild their self-esteem and autonomy. Develop, train and coach them to make them feel capable again, lead them in an honourable way, give them time, attention, recognition and appreciation and you will make them feel loveable and included.

The ultimate goal of a leader in a neglected organisation will be to train and develop the employees so that they can thrive. As parents do, leaders might lean towards various 'parenting' styles:

- **Authoritarian:** strict – there is no room for discussion and no explanations are given. There is one choice: obey. This does not stimulate growth and learning.

- **Authoritative:** both responsive and demanding. The caregiver is involved in helping to solve problems and pays a lot of attention to the feelings of the child. Crossing the line has consequences and explanations are given to help learning. There are clear rules and the child is (increasingly) allowed to take decisions. This creates predictability, increases trust and fairness, stimulates learning and builds self-confidence.

- **Laissez-faire:** warm and involved but also detached and distant. The child does not get enough attention and there are no clear boundaries. The child feels ignored and unimportant and can't rely on the caregiver so tries to take care of herself/himself but is not equipped to do so.

The authoritative style is the most effective for curing neglect in organisations. It is a combination of giving clear directions and encouraging more participation and ownership. There is lots of attention to feelings and wellbeing but also clear boundaries, predictable processes and balancing of the organisation's goals and needs with those of the individual. This is a style that creates an environment of trust and fairness, stimulates learning and growth and builds self-confidence.

Leadership for turning around businesses

In my quest to find the most effective leadership styles for transformations and turnarounds – the ones that tackle organisational pathologies – I found two theories that have consistently delivered good results.

Level 5 leadership

'Level 5 leadership' was introduced by Jim Collins in his book *Good to Great*.[23] He analysed 1,435 companies over forty years to discover the type of leadership that helped companies move ahead and deliver sustainable results. Only eleven companies (from the 1,435) kept delivering. Their leadership shared certain characteristics.

The leaders came from within the organisation, were both strong-willed (and passionate) and humble, were normal people without big egos, and were highly capable individuals, contributing team members and competent managers. They were ambitious for the organisation rather than for themselves and fanatically driven to produce exceptional results on a sustainable basis. They built successors to be even more successful than they were. They shared praise and took responsibility and blame.

To develop Level 5 leadership in your organisation, you need to recruit from within and select people with the three I's who are top performers in their area. They need to be emotionally intelligent, ambitious and humble, able to lead with passion and drive, and develop loyal followers. If you can find these people you have a good start.

---

23   J Collins, *Good to Great: Why some companies make the leap... and others don't* (Random House, 2001)

Servant leadership

Robert K Greenleaf is the first person who used 'servant leadership' in business in 1970 in his essay 'The servant as a leader',[24] but this concept has existed since ancient times.

Servant leadership is a holistic and positive leadership approach that inverts the norm. Instead of the people working to serve the leader, the leader exists to serve the people. Where traditional leadership generally involves the accumulation and exercise of power by one person at the apex of the pyramid, here the power comes from the base.

Servant leaders are ethical and altruistic leaders who focus on developing people, building a trusting team and achieving results. They lead with vision, are honest, have high integrity and trust and put service first. They are role models and pioneers who appreciate and empower others. The characteristics of servant leaders according to Greenleaf are:

- Leading from a why

- Listening

- Empathy

- Healing

- Awareness

---

24 RK Greenleaf, 'The servant as leader' (pamphlet, 1970)

- Persuasion

- Conceptualisation

- Foresight

- Stewardship

- Commitment to the growth of people

- Building community

Servant leaders share power, put the needs of employees first and help them develop and perform as highly as possible. They see themselves as stewards who are entrusted to develop and empower followers to reach their full potential. They focus on the needs of others, especially team members, before their own. They include, acknowledge and support people to meet their work and personal goals, involve them in decisions where appropriate, and build a sense of community within their teams. This leads to higher engagement, more trust, and stronger relationships with team members and other stakeholders.

The leaders' main task is to help their people grow: to become healthier, wiser, freer, more autonomous – and become servant leaders themselves. When employees grow, the organisation grows as well due to the employees' growing commitment and engagement. A servant leader focuses primarily on the growth and wellbeing of people and the communities to which they belong.

Servant leadership transforms businesses because:

- It creates reciprocity: because you care for your leadership team, they care for the employees and stakeholders. Positivity trickles down in the organisation. (Fixing your management team fast is key to making this possible.)

- The employees feel a sense of trust and a need to return their employer's commitment to the organisation, which in turn increases the brand perception and reduces employee job turnover.

- Employees who have positive experiences and satisfaction at work bring positive energy home and thus start improving their communities.

- It contributes to employees' goal achievement and success. Employees feel supported to grow and become better people.

- If employees' needs are prioritised and they sense that they have social support from their leader as well as their colleagues, they are more likely to be engaged in their work.

- A climate of understanding and forgiveness creates safety and helps employees learn from their mistakes, change unhelpful behaviour and grow as people.

- Servant leaders are seen as good role models in the eyes of their employees, who begin to act as servant leaders themselves.

Summary

This chapter highlighted the importance of the sustainable alignment of your management team, including how to choose your people, the leadership style that works for organisations that have suffered neglect and the leadership style you need for turning businesses around.

The focus in this chapter was not on talking your team into alignment but on changing how the business is led, facilitating the healing of the enterprise and putting a positive leadership in place with values that will trickle down in your organisation and enable your business to not only survive but thrive.

Now that you have your team aligned to your mission, we will move on to discuss planning and vision.

8

Building Block 4 – Future Vision And Plan

During the Fix, Reset and Accelerate programme keep the following in mind: the ambition, vision, strategy, business model and earning model of your business. You will need to understand all these things as you embark on your turnaround journey, set up the monitoring of your business and perform your diagnosis. Don't spend time in your meetings on theoretical discussions about what the strategic terms mean. Get on with the steps and it will become clear.

After five months in the Fix phase, having taken the right steps to fix your performance and profitability, you will be moving towards your break-even point and seeing your financials improving steadily every month. You are ready for the Reset phase.

At this point you will work on defining your new strategy, earning model and business model, and developing a plan for sustainably transforming your business. In this step you will need to consider the impact of the Fourth Industrial Revolution, the UN's Sustainable Global Goals and the Great Reset on the future of your company and include them in your plan to make your business thrive.

What you will do in the Reset phase:

- Return to the holistic model (Chapter 4) to ensure that you don't forget any part of your business

- Maintain the monitoring process you set up in the Fix phase and set up additional metrics to monitor the business after you have made the planned changes

- Reaffirm the alignment of your management team and improve your team dynamics

- Position your new hero army to help you translate your new strategy into plans and action and lead projects under the supervision of a management team member and a project management office

- Make detailed execution plans, allocating projects to management team members/owners and project managers, setting up a project management office, and agreeing processes for governance, decision-making and communication and required consultation with employee representatives

- Inform your entire organisation about the plans, get feedback and engagement and work out how to keep people informed

In this chapter I will show you in a simple and systematic way to define your future business vision by assessing your market, defining your strategy and putting your strategy into action.

You will define your strategy, business model and earning model but they will always be beta versions as the environment will keep changing and you will constantly need to adjust to new information. Don't go for perfect; be directionally right and be prepared to act fast, fail fast and learn fast. That's how you create success for your business from an entrepreneurial perspective.

The key things to remember in this phase are to:

- Have thorough strategic conversations (rather than getting lost in jargon and difficult discussions about definitions)

- Use reliable sources and information

- Keep a helicopter view

- Push relentlessly for progress from strategy definition to full implementation

Strategy implementation succeeds when you manage to involve your entire company in reviewing the defined strategy and in the implementation. As with the P&L, the strategy and goals will need to be cascaded from company level to functional area level and individual level. Everyone needs to be clear about their role in the strategy implementation. This increases the alignment of functional areas and individual goals to company-wide goals and increases motivation in the company. When your contribution matters and you see it positively impacting the future of your company, you are more motivated.

The following step-by-step approach to strategy development and implementation is based on various existing strategy and transformation models that have worked for me in turnaround and transformation projects. I integrated these into this seven key steps model (step five has two parts):

1. Understand the impact of market developments

2. Decide on the ambition and the why of your business

3. Create a business and earning model

4. Translate strategy into a set of requirements for your business model

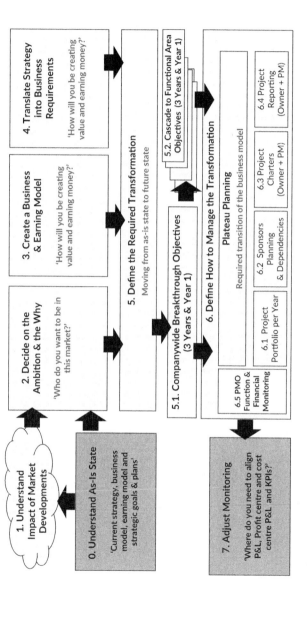

Developing your future vision

5. Define the required transformation (from as-is to future state) by:

   – Defining breakthrough organisation-wide objectives (for three years and one year)

   – Cascading the company-wide objectives to functional area objectives

6. Define how to manage the transformation

7. Adjust the company monitoring to reflect the new objectives

Let's look at how to carry out each of the steps in turn.

Understand the impact of market developments

When you understand the impact of market developments, you will be able to take educated business decisions while defining your strategy.

Looking outside in

Look first at the political, economic, social and technological factors affecting your market and/or industry. What is their impact on your company, sales, cost level, competition, growth and margin?

Analysis of external factors

Competitive analysis

This simplified Porter's Five Forces model allows you insight into how to beat or avoid competition, and how to find new business opportunities and use them to generate more revenues and avoid investing in areas with increased competition.[25]

---

25 Adapted from the Porter Five Forces Framework (Michael E. Porter, 'How Competitive Forces Shape Strategy', *Harvard Business Review*, 1979, 57(2), 137–145)

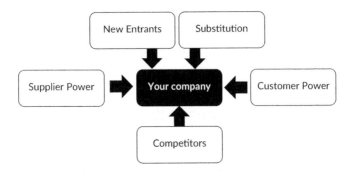

Competitive analysis

It means analysing, in turn, supplier power, customer power, competitors, substitution and new entrants.

Supplier power

How many core suppliers do you have? Can you switch suppliers easily and reduce overall cost? How high are your switching costs? Are you dependent on specific suppliers? Can they increase their cost and damage your margin? How unique are their products or services? What happens if they start working with your competitor or selling via a direct channel?

Customer power

How many clients do you have? How significant are they in terms of purchasing volumes? Can they push down the price and damage your margin? How expensive is it for them to switch to your competitor?

Competitors

How many competitors do you have? Who are they and how does the quality of their products and services compare with yours? What does this competition mean for your prices and marketing efforts? What does this mean for your profitability and margin? How probable is it that your clients and suppliers will start working with your competitors? What do you need to do to counter this competition?

Substitution

How easy would it be for customers to replace your products and services with something else?

New entrants

How easy is it for new players to enter your market? What are the costs involved? How tight are the regulations and compliance demands?

Strengths, weaknesses, opportunities and threats

When a company moves from focusing on weaknesses and threats to focusing on using its strengths to exploit emerging opportunities, it will start shifting its investments to services/products and niches and markets that will enable it to grow and thrive. This SWOT analysis will help you uncover your company's strengths, weaknesses, opportunities and threats.

Strengths, weaknesses, opportunities
and threats

Strengths

What sets you apart from your competitors – know-how, technology, people skills, reputation, other factors?

Weaknesses

What internal factors are holding back your quality, competitiveness and financial outcomes? Think systems, speed of innovation, low productivity, quality of service, high cost base, weak operations, quality of IT, compliance, ability to scale up, quality of marketing and ability to sell.

Opportunities

How are your strengths generating opportunities for your business? Which segments and markets can you service with your strengths, given favourable external developments in your market and local / global policies?

Threats

What threats are your weaknesses generating for your business? Which ones (if not addressed) could impact your business and earning model? Think about adaptation to environment and trends and new regulations, competition and compliance.

Decide on the ambition and the why

Craft your 'why' statement. It should be simple, short and easy to understand. Focus on why your business exists. What you do to generate (unique) value at this stage is not important.

Ask yourself: what is your compelling purpose as a business that inspires you? Is it at the core of everything you do in your business? When is your business at its best? What are you passionate about? What is the core purpose of your business in society? Why does it matter?

Spotify's why, for instance, is 'to unlock the potential of human creativity – by giving a million creative artists the opportunity to live off their art and billions of fans the opportunity to enjoy and be inspired by it'.[26]

Southwestern Airlines' why is to 'connect people to what's important in their lives through friendly, reliable, and low-cost air travel'.[27]

Once you have settled on your why, define in which region, countries or niches you want to do this activity in for least the next three years.

Create a business and earning model

Now that you have studied the impact of market developments on your business, the impact of competition on its products and services, found its market opportunities and threats and defined the (revised) ambition and the why, the next step is to define your new futureproof business and earning model.

For that we will use the business model map below.

---

26 K Fagan, 'Spotify's 35-year-old co-founder wrote an emotional letter to investors…' *Business Insider*, 2018
27 Southwestern Airlines website, www.southwest.com/html/about-southwest/index.html

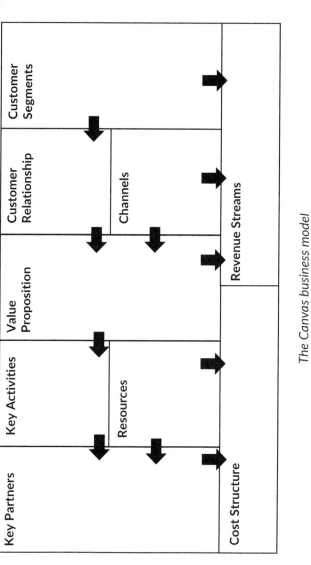

The Canvas business model
(Adapted from Canvas tool in A Osterwalder and Y Pigneur, *Business Model Generation*, Wiley, 2010)

We will define the areas of this business model map by answering the following questions:

- **Customer segments:** for which customers / clients are we creating value? Who are your most important customers? Are you targeting a mass market, niche market, a segmented market, a diversified market or a multi-sided platform?

- **Customer relationship:** what type of relationship does each of your customer segments expect you to establish and maintain with them (automated services, self-service, full support)? Which relationship types are already in place? How are they integrated in your business model? How costly is it to maintain these types of relationships?

- **Channels:** through which channels do your customer segments want to be reached? How are you reaching them now? How are your channels integrated? Which ones work best? Which ones are most cost-efficient? How are they integrated in your current servicing model?

- **Value proposition:** what value do you deliver to your customer / client? Which of your customers' problems are you helping to solve? What set of products and services are you offering to each customer segment? Which customer needs are you already satisfying (price, quality, availability, selection, functionality, service, brand/image, innovation, partnership)?

- **Revenue streams:** for what value are your customers willing to pay? For what do they currently pay? How are they currently paying? How would they prefer to pay? How much does each revenue stream contribute to overall revenues? You will have to consider types of revenues and both fixed and dynamic pricing. Types of revenues: asset sale, usage fee, subscription fees, lending/renting/leasing, licensing, brokerage fees, advertising. Types of fixed pricing: list price, product feature dependent, customer segment dependent, volume dependent. Types of dynamic pricing: negotiation, yield management, real-time-market.

- **Key activities:** what key activities do you need to deliver your value proposition? Your distribution channels? Your customer relationships? Your revenue streams? For each activity think through the three P's: process, platform, people.

- **Key resources:** what key resources are needed for your value propositions? Your distribution channels? Your customer relationships? Your revenue streams? Think through types of resources: physical, intellectual (brand patents, copyrights, data), human and financial.

- **Key partners:** who are your key partners? Who are your key suppliers? Which key resources are you acquiring from partners? Which key activities do partners perform? (Partners are interested in economies of scale, reduction of risk and uncertainty and acquiring of particular know-how, intellectual property, resources and activities.)

- **Cost structure:** what are the costs for your business model? Which key resources are required and what are the fully loaded costs of these resources? What are the key activities and what are the costs involved? Are you an efficiency-driven business (lean structure, low price, maximum automation and extensive outsourcing) or a value-driven business with the focus on value creation, premium value proposition and customer intimacy?

Translate strategy into business requirements

So far we have defined our ambition and why, market developments and how they are impacting the business, how we will use our strengths and opportunities to gain competitive advantage and, finally, how we want to add value and what our business and earning model should be.

We now move on to defining the strategic priorities and goals and requirements for the entire business by using a strategy map, defined by Kaplan and Norton in their book *The Balanced Scorecard*.[28]

This defines the business requirements for transforming the business at four levels: from a financial perspective, a customer/client perspective, an internal perspective and a learning and growth perspective.

Financial perspective

How do you want to create long-term value for your shareholders?

- A growth strategy (expanding revenue opportunities and enhancing customer value)

- A productivity strategy (improving cost structure and increasing asset utilisation)

- A growth and productivity strategy (I recommend this option in a turnaround)

Customer perspective

Are you creating value for your customers/clients through:

- Product/service attributes (price, quality, availability, selection, functionality)?

---

28 RS Kaplan and DP Norton, *The Balanced Scorecard: Translating strategy into action* (Harvard Business Review Press, 1996)

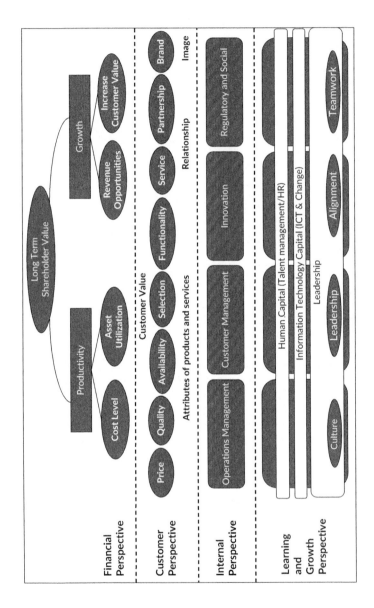

The strategy map

- Relationship: service and partnership?
- Image: reputation/brand?

If you can combine all three you will be winning.

Internal perspective

To reach your strategic objectives, what are the strategic goals that you want to give to each key process (and functional area)?

- Operations management (supply, production, distribution, risk management)
- Customer management (selection, acquisition, retention, growth)
- Innovation (opportunity identification, R&D port-folio, design development, launch)
- Regulatory and social (environment, safety and health, employment and community)

Learning and growth perspective

What are the strategic goals that you want to give to each enabler to reach your strategic objectives?

- Human capital (for your talent management team/HR)

- Information (technology) capital (for your ICT and change team)

- Organisational capital: culture, leadership, alignment and teamwork (for the leadership and talent management)

Define the required transformation

After following steps 1 to 4, you will see that there is a gap between where the business currently is (the as-is) and where it needs to go (its future state). A transition or transformation will be required to get to the future state. You need to set goals for your business and all its functional areas through goal-setting in two stages – first setting company-wide breakthrough objectives, then cascading these objectives and their structured implementation through the functional areas.

Company-wide breakthrough objectives

Set breakthrough objectives for each of the four per-spectives discussed above (financial, customer / client, internal, learning and growth). The breakthrough objectives should be formulated for the coming three years and be deduced for the coming year. Below is a handy checklist of breakthrough objectives to build on and customise, including allocation to the departments that should own them.

Perspective	Draft breakthrough goals for three years and per year	Responsible
Financial	Revenue growth	Sales
	Reduction of the relative cost level	Ops
Customer	Improve product/service attributes	All
	• Price	
	• Quality	
	• Availability	
	• Selection	
	• Functionality	
	Improve relationship	All
	• Service	
	• Partnership	
	Improve image	Marketing + All
	• Brand recognition	
	• Brand awareness	
	• Brand loyalty	
Internal	Improve operations management processes	Ops
	• Supply, production, distribution, risk management	
	• Quality of service	
	• Efficiency	

Perspective	Draft breakthrough goals for three years and per year	Responsible
Internal	Improve customer management	Sales + Ops
	• Increase winning deal	
	• Client acquisition	
	• Retention	
	• Growth	
	Improve innovation processes	R&D
	• Efficiency and effectiveness	
	• Time to market	
	• Conformance to budget and time	
	• Customer satisfaction post-launch	
	Improve regulatory and social processes	Finance + Risk
	• Risk management	
	• Nullifying exposures and claims	
Learning and growth	Develop human capital to deliver new proposition	Talent Management + All
	• Within X months	
	Information (technology) capital	IT + Change + All
	• Have the systems and support ready	

Perspective	Draft breakthrough goals for three years and per year	Responsible
Learning and growth	Organisational capital (culture, leadership, alignment and teamwork)	MD + Talent Management + All
	• Improve employee satisfaction and engagement	
	• Increase retention	
	• Increase health	

Cascade to functional area objectives

The next step is straightforward. The three years' and next year's objectives will need to be owned by the management team. Every management team member will need to discuss with their team how their goals will be achieved and put a high-level plan in place that should include: initiatives, timelines, required resources, risks and mitigations, and names of the talented team members who will project manage each initiative under the responsibility of the management team member. These talented individuals will already be part of your hero army.

Areas with shared owners will need to collaborate; one of the management team members becomes the key owner and the others will be sponsoring and contributing. The input of the management team members will be discussed first in a one-to-one with the MD, then brought to the management table. The MD should be watching over the dependencies and quality of the plans.

Once the breakthrough goals have been finalised, the management team members will need to translate them to their managers and thereafter their employees so that everybody gets a role in the execution of the business strategy.

Define how to manage the transformation

The defined initiatives for implementing the strategy must be governed by a portfolio, a list of all initiatives that will include for each one: the owner (and sponsor), project manager, key timelines, required resources, budget, risks and mitigations.

If there are many initiatives with significant budget and resources, you will need a project management office role: someone experienced in project management and project monitoring who will facilitate the process, help with standardising project charters (plans) and project reporting, set up a reporting and monitoring process for all initiatives and work closely with finance to set up financial monitoring of the projects. This person will support the management team during the entire implementation. The project management office should be set up during the Reset phase and continue during the Accelerate phase to monitor the execution of the projects (and thereby strategy implementation).

In the Accelerate phase, the management team will need to meet every week to review the progress of the entire project portfolio (pushed through via the PMO), take required decisions, remove bottlenecks and facilitate the project managers, project owners and teams. Once this starts flowing, as everybody is owning their part, progress will be made quickly. Alignment, a good and coherent plan, a good structure, scaling up execution power, good monitoring and reporting and timely decision-making will transform the business.

In Chapter 11, about predictable process, you will learn how to manage the entire Fix, Reset and Accelerate programme in a way that distributes accountability, keeps people on board with the company turnaround and delivers timely results.

Adjust the company monitoring

You might find that your breakthrough goals and initiatives affect the KPIs you defined in the Fix phase. It will be essential to review these after setting your breakthrough goals and adjusting where required. You don't want to lose the grip that you now have over the business once performance has improved.

Summary

In this chapter we discussed how to assess your market, define your strategy and bring your strategy into execution. We introduced a pragmatic step-by-step approach to understanding (relevant) market developments, competition and your strengths, weaknesses, opportunities and threats. We decided on the ambition and 'why' of the business; created a business and earning model; translated strategy into a set of requirements for your business model; defined the steps for the required transformation through breakthrough objectives that are then cascaded to all functional areas; and discussed how to manage the transformation from the as-is to the future state.

The next chapter will look at how you can deploy the talent in your organisation to best advantage to help you achieve all this.

9

Building Block 5 – Unleashing Talent

I had a lucky break when I was twenty-two. I was hired by an American consulting firm with 55,000 employees around the globe, which saw developing talent as key to gaining competitive advantage. Their slogan was 'Happy people produce quality'.

The company was not hierarchical; everyone felt heard, respected, included and appreciated. It was fair; you needed to earn the great assignments by selling your services (at interviews with your own salespeople and clients) and over-delivering. The rewards were not only increased remuneration but also better assignments, training and personal growth. The sky was the limit for your potential. When you did well, the business did well (in terms of client satisfaction and fees) – a great win-win.

When you joined the company, your manager, also your coach, would ask you to take an MBTI talent assessment (discussed in Chapter 3). The test gave you and your coach insights into what made you unique. This was used as a strong foundation for the selection of your assignments and your development journey. The company operated from the principle that when you do what you are best at you will always excel.

This worked well for me. I am still grateful for the coaching and opportunities I received during my four years there. The company was one of my best employers. I worked with amazing colleagues – happy people who were doing well – and my manager checked every month how I was doing and how he could help me develop and grow. As talent in that company, you were the driving force behind your own personal development and you had the support to get where you wanted to go, in alignment with the company's goals.

We had an inspiring female CEO in the US, who visited our branch every now and then, had lunch with us and had a normal chat, with zero ego, about how things were going. We had a weekly get-together on Fridays and annual whole-company trips. I loved working there, I loved the company, worked as hard as if it was my own business, advanced fast and had fun. This experience in my early career shaped my perception of work, talent, talent management and unleashing human potential.

Working for other clients, I discovered that this was not the norm. At the majority of companies for which I did transformation projects or turnarounds, people were hired to do a job. No one cared about their opinion or development – they were doing the same job for years, they worked from nine to five and some were walking dead. Some bosses were tyrants (those silverback gorillas again), freaking their people out, yelling at them, telling them to keep their 'stupid' opinions to themselves. These companies had low morale, poor results and low engagement.

Unleashing talent to Fix, Reset and Accelerate

When I was hired to help businesses fix performance or get things done – because, they claimed, their own people were not smart enough – I needed only to reverse the madness that was going on, the assault on human potential and talent. Once I had unleashed the talent in the company I achieved great results, often within one to two months. The answer is always with people, by developing people and through people. That is where the magic happens in the Fix, Reset and Accelerate approach, when you find, heal, develop and unleash the talent in the company, direct it towards a great collective why, and empower people through guidance, coaching, praise, rewards and great opportunities.

In every transformation or turnaround assignment I do, I am always scouting talent. I want to have the best people on my core team. I facilitate them to do their MBTI and find their talent and their voice and help them rebuild their self-esteem (feeling loveable, capable and part of a family). I mentor them, arrange development programmes and teach them what I know to help them develop and grow.

If you select the right people, you get back ten-fold what you invest in terms of trust, loyalty, dedication, results, belonging, fun and developing other people around them. Everyone you develop will go on to develop five to ten other people. It is amazing to see this positive vibe trickling down through the organisation.

This chapter identifies why talent will be so important in the next decade, what you need to change in your business to keep and attract talent, how to identify management talent and young talent, and how to unleash the talent in your company to make use of its full potential.

Why talent will be important in the coming years

As discussed in Chapter 1, we are in the middle of a global transformation. Talent, leadership, culture and structures will have to be rethought. Companies will need to re-examine the way they do business.

Business leaders and senior executives will need to understand the Fourth Industrial Revolution, monitor their changing environment, reassess their processes with their teams and continuously innovate to survive and thrive in these changing times.

We discussed also that talent, rather than capital, will become businesses' most important asset. Shortages in talent can be expected in the market. Businesses will need to continuously develop their own (extended) teams. Education of the company's leadership and talent needs to focus on capabilities to effectively interact and execute in ecosystems and deliver new value; on developing entrepreneurial talent and mindset; as well as on the adaptation and transformation skills needed to keep up with the speed of this next industrial revolution. Businesses need agile collaboration models and top-down decision-making will no longer work.

To thrive in this age, you will need to have the best talent and you will need to develop and keep them. You need also to have a critical mass of talent to turn your business around fast and win in your market.

What you need to change

Your company's why matters

We talked in the previous chapter about the why of your business: the compelling purpose that inspires you and lies at the core of everything you do. The why that underlies the passion of the business and its unique contribution to society. Talent is attracted to an awesome why and to the contribution they can make to achieving it. They can get the paycheque anywhere, so they want to work for the right why. Get your authentic why right, communicate it well and you will become a talent magnet.

Be a chief talent sponsor

Great leaders are passionate about talent, like they are passionate about capital. Without it you can't grow your business. Get involved in hiring, welcoming, rating, scouting, nominating, developing and keeping your talent. These people will make your business thrive. Keep them close, meet and interact with them regularly and listen to what they have to say.

If you do this, they will know how important they are for your company and for you. They will understand your business strategy and what they should be doing to make the best contribution.

Change the rules

Talent is your ticket to win in the decades to come. Don't let old organisational mistakes destroy that ticket. The boss/slave hierarchy that has been created in companies is an assault on human potential and talent and departments have become walls that protect turf, stop collaboration and block talent.

We need to pull down those mental walls, treat everyone as talent with human potential, align their signature (core talent) and development needs with company goals and make sure they feel heard, seen and appreciated.

The leaders of the pack also need to be pack members, sharing the collective risks. They need to earn their rank while leading the way. Unleashing talent means that everybody is equal, that silverback gorillas and their egos are no longer welcome; it means that we install respect, equality, fairness and servant leadership. It means we become genuinely interested in people as whole people, not resources.

HR becomes talent management and development

In all turnarounds I do, I work intensively with the management team member responsible for the people department. You probably know this as HR – human resources – but I don't like that name. People are not resources. People have talent. I prefer to call it talent management and development.

When I arrive, this department is not taken seriously; they do admin, pay salaries, take care of sickness registration and do recruiting when needed for the managers. They are not seen as an exciting department.

I always start a turnaround with financials, KPIs and people. We start putting this department where it belongs, next to the CFO. Talent is as important as capital; you should make this process as important as your budgeting process. I make sure talent management gets a strategy, key drivers (KPIs) and a formalised hiring process in order to start focusing on enabling management and talent, talent growth, engagement, satisfaction, and health and reward.

At Microsoft they know that a top software developer is 10,000 times more productive than an average software developer.[29] This is why talent matters and why the quality of your entire team matters.

The talent management and development department (formerly known as HR) will therefore need to facilitate at the start of the Fix phase, in close collaboration with the managing director, a fair and transparent review of all employees with their managers. All reviews will be challenged at the management team table, employee representatives will be involved and they will feed back about the process.

---

29 J McMillan, 'Top software developers are 10,000 times more productive – really?', McMillanTech, no date, www.mcmillantech. co.uk/wordpress_0/software-companies/top-software-developers

Every person in the organisation, including the management team members and managers, will be allocated a rating ranging from 1 to 5.

Rating	Performance	Talent management action
1	Overperformer	Senior – develop and grow towards a leadership position
		Pay above market and keep
2	High performer	Develop and grow towards senior position
		Pay above market and keep
3	Average performer	Appreciate, keep and grow
		Give market-conforming pay
4	Underperformer	Coach to recover in three months
		If keeps underperforming, move to band 5
5	Structural underperformer	Damaging the business: needs to leave

This exercise will provide insight into the top 15% talent of the business, the ones that will help you haul the rest of the company through change. This is your hero army: the people who will need to go through your development programme during the first six months of the Fix, Reset and Accelerate project, who in six months will start running the strategic initiatives discussed in the previous chapter. Ensure they are evenly distributed over all functional areas. If you don't have any 1 or 2 ratings in a particular department, you will need to hire them.

With this exercise we also identify those who are causing quality issues in the business (ratings 4 and 5). When you ask people with rating 5 to leave your business, do it in an honourable way. Mistakes were made by the business in the hiring process and these individuals went through probation and stayed. They were probably doing this work for years, knowing they were not doing well, and nobody helped them to improve or leave. They are victims in this situation. Reimburse them according to local law, apologise for the process, seek understanding and let them depart in an honourable way. Here again you are setting a leadership example.

How to identify management and young talent

We discussed in the building block on management alignment that to make businesses thrive you will need to work on the quality of your management team, selecting them based on the three I's (intelligence, integrity and 'I can do it' attitude). They should be top notch in their functional area, good with their financials, understand IT and be able to run projects. They need also to have good people skills and be transformational leaders.

We also discussed the most effective leadership styles for transformations and turnarounds – those that tackle organisational pathologies: Level 5 leadership and servant leadership, combined with an authoritative management style.

Building a great organisation that keeps, develops, attracts and unleashes talent means that all management and talent in the organisation, who will start leading others in strategic initiatives, need to have the same DNA.

Management talent

One of the issues you will face in turnarounds and transformations is the quality of the middle management. When you find 4 and 5 ratings in middle management, they have to go.

According to research by Tom Peters (in his book *Talent*), Georgia Pacific replaced twenty of their forty managers with more talented, higher paid people and were able to increase their market cap by 50% in three years.[30]

Your management should have ratings of 1 and 2. Check them on the three I's; they should be top-notch professionals and they should have great people skills. These people are developable. They can learn the other skills in the development programme of Fix, Reset and Accelerate.

---

30   T Peters, *Talent* (DK, 2005)

Once you have developed your managers, give them a mentoring role and rate (and reward) them, next to hitting financial targets and KPIs, on the development, growth and performance of their people and on building future leaders.

Young talent

Ensure that the talent selected for your hero army is diverse: select from all functional areas, personality types, ages, educational backgrounds and cultures, and balance the number of men and women in the group.

The talented people are usually non-conformists, rebels, eccentrics; they are fun to be around, they are go-getters, bold and often young and they believe in changing the world. They have great energy, are thrilled by challenges and love getting things done.

Enable them to discover their greatness using MBTI, give them awesome projects, develop them, set sky-high standards, pay them well, focus on their growth, give them young management assignments (as in the Fix, Reset and Accelerate programme), remove communication barriers, give them guidance, coaching, praise, rewards and great opportunities. When the opportunity is there, and they are ready, promote them to management and leadership positions.

How to unleash the talent in your company

Scouting talent, allocating people to projects that match their talent and giving them proper and relevant education will allow you to build your entire Fix, Reset and Accelerate hero army in around six months, which will help you accelerate the transformation of your business.

If done in a targeted way, this development should not cost a lot. The people you upskill and right-skill will be contributing to your programme from an early stage and will be the future leaders of your strategic initiatives and later leaders in your business. Investing in your people will increase loyalty and quality of outcomes (in operations and projects) and will save you money on hiring expensive (temporary) consultants and professionals for leadership roles in the (near) future.

How many people do you need in your hero army? Around 15% of your people, with ratings of 1 and 2, evenly distributed over all departments and organisational levels (directors, managers and employees). This population should be distributed as follows: 15% top management, 30% middle management and 55% talent.

These people should be the most talented, qualified and respected people in their teams. They will become the energy starters through your whole company and the ones who will bring others along. When you can't find a potential recruit for your hero army in a department, fix that gap. That's an urgent quality problem.

These people will be your winning league: put them in charge of all your strategic projects once you have developed them and you will have a money and growth machine.

Summary

Talent will be vital in the years to come so change what you need to in your company to keep and attract talent, to identify management and young talent, and to unleash the talent already within your company.

The next chapter establishes the skills that leadership, managers and talent should be equipped with to achieve maximum results in a Fix, Reset and Accelerate programme.

10
Building Block 6 – Turnaround DNA

The people in your hero army will themselves need support to help you transform your business and carry the rest of the company through change.

You will need a turnaround and transformation programme that will directly help your top 15% to effectively contribute to improving profitability, resetting the strategy, the positioning, earning and business model, accelerating the implementation of the new strategic objectives and thereby moving your business faster than the competitors towards the conditions that will make it thrive.

After years of observing executives, management teams, managers and talent in turnaround and transformation projects, I came to see which skills were most helpful in developing transformational leaders. The result is my Turnaround and Transformation DNA Programme.

The skills your hero army needs

Today the curriculum of the Turnaround and Transformation DNA Programme consists of the following:

- Talent scouting and development (finding their own signature and core talent)

- Understanding the future (economic, policy and technological developments)

- Leading through times of crisis and all-pervasive change

- Understanding how to Fix, Reset and Accelerate a business in twelve months

- Understanding finance turnaround and transformation

- Understanding talent management (ex-HR) turnaround and transformation

- Understanding operational performance improvement and transformation

- Organising for success

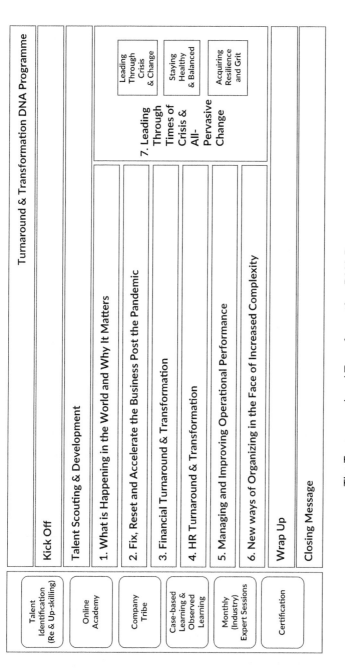

Turnaround & Transformation DNA Programme

Talent Identification (Re & Up-skilling)	Kick Off		
Online Academy	Talent Scouting & Development		
Company Tribe	1. What is Happening in the World and Why It Matters		
	2. Fix, Reset and Accelerate the Business Post the Pandemic		
Case-based Learning & Observed Learning	3. Financial Turnaround & Transformation		
	4. HR Turnaround & Transformation		
Monthly (Industry) Expert Sessions	5. Managing and Improving Operational Performance		
	6. New ways of Organizing in the Face of Increased Complexity		
	7. Leading Through Times of Crisis & All-Pervasive Change	Leading Through Crisis & Change
			Staying Healthy & Balanced
			Acquiring Resilience and Grit
Certification	Wrap Up		
	Closing Message		

The Turnaround and Transformation DNA Programme

- Developing the leadership, resilience and grit that are required during times of crisis and transformation

Focus of the Turnaround DNA Programme

The Turnaround and Transformation DNA Programme has become a practical mini-MBA in six months. If you start running this for your hero army they will apply their skills right away for your business's benefit and will be able to manage and effectively contribute to turnarounds and transformations.

I based the content of these modules on what I learned in my MBA plus my lengthy experience of solving issues during turnaround and transformation programmes. I draw on a range of influences and resources ranging from psychology to governance, managing successful programmes, the Lean and Six Sigma business programmes, and my wider studies in leadership, turnaround management, human behaviour, resilience, health and personal development.

In every business I have worked with, I have focused on identifying people with exceptional abilities and leadership potential, reskilling and upskilling them and setting up multifunctional (virtual) cohorts that represent all departments of the organisation (at executive, management and employee level). These cohorts formed tribes in their specific companies. I have set up a Turnaround and Transformation Academy to help them to build their knowledge. I give them assignments based on real company cases to increase collaboration. We hold monthly sessions to interact, allow participants to ask questions and learn from peers. I recently moved this academy, with my team, to an online format to enable participants to study from home. I set exams and issue certificates to ensure that people get a sense of achievement from it.

Running a programme like this, or with similar components, will help you embed these skills in the top 15% of your company at all three levels: executives, managers and talents. These people will be influencers in your company, creating a common language, connecting and aligning talent from all departments around the transformation goals of the Fix, Reset and Accelerate programme. They will increase the pace and quality of execution of both your business and your turnaround programme.

The team will learn so much over the six months and will grow in confidence, see more, understand more and contribute more. Personal development, combined with new knowledge and skills, has a great impact on people. You are working to help your company to find their unique talent, unleash it, prove themselves, gain visibility, get the appreciation they deserve and rebuild their self-esteem.

Summary

The Turnaround DNA Programme is the means by which you empower your top 15% to become an effective and forward-thinking hero army of transformational leaders. We discussed the key turnaround and transformation skills it should include, what it should focus on and how it will make your key players more effective.

In the next chapter I will show you the overall picture of the Fix, Reset and Accelerate method and its building blocks and tell you how you can bring it together into a predictable process for your organisation. This will help you share the narrative about the what, how and when of what you are doing with your team, organisation and stakeholders.

11
Building Block 7 –
Predictable Process

A turnaround programme is a lot for any organisation to deal with. You are working to fix an organisation in crisis that has suffered neglect and is stuck in harmful patterns. You have to address the concerns of worried stakeholders (employee representatives, clients, suppliers, shareholders, banks and supervisors); keep the going concern running; and while turning around the business to improve its profitability, resetting its strategy and building new capabilities to accelerate its competitive ability. You will be completely refurbishing a shop while the sales are on.

In this process, you will be asking your people to walk a tightrope from what they know (and that no longer serves the business but still feels familiar) towards the unknown. Everything is new and scary and will make them feel anxious. It is your responsibility as leader to show them the way, reduce uncertainty and help them grow. When you need to take decisions that will heavily rock the boat, you will need to keep your people informed and explain your rationale.

You need an act of faith from your shareholders. They need to trust you and support you in the process and they will only do that if you know what you are doing, involve them and make them your advisers.

This will involve juggling with lots of balls for at least a year before you can start normalising the business again. A structured and systematic approach will help you stay on top of things, give the helicopter view you need and help you plan meetings to mobilise your team, organisation and stakeholders. Manage your schedule and the schedule of your team. You need to stop the 'rocking chair' meetings (lots of movement, going nowhere). You and your people will need to free up time to run the going concern and the turnaround at the same time.

In this chapter I will share with you how I structure my programmes using a simple step-by-step model. When a lot is going on, we tend to lose the helicopter view and the detail of what needs to happen. I start with the helicopter view and deliverables before the turnaround work really kicks in.

This model will help you simplify your Fix, Reset and Accelerate programme, manage the involvement of your stakeholders, keep monitoring the profitability and performance of the business, ensure timely decision-making with your management team and manage the big changes that need to happen and the flow of communication. You will be able to keep on top of the turnaround phases, their deliverables and how employees are feeling during the process.

Using this structure to keep your team and organisation informed enables people to understand what is happening and that they have a role and can make a positive contribution. Once they are kept informed, they tend to relax and engage positively with the programme.

Helicopter view of the programme

This chart summarises the steps that need to be taken in the programme. We will explain the elements below.

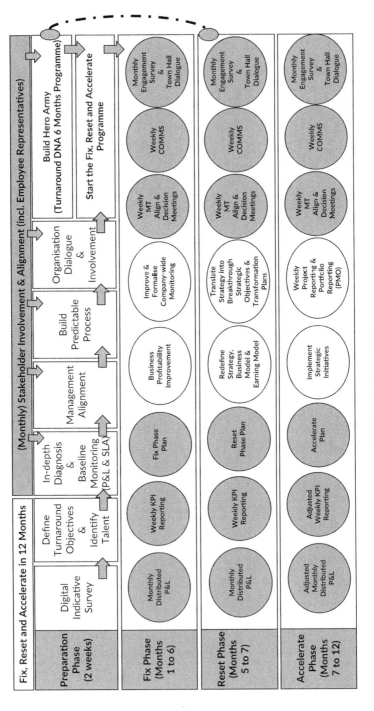

Helicopter view of the programme

Monthly stakeholder involvement and alignment meetings

A useful practice is to organise regular meetings with your employee representatives, key clients, key suppliers, shareholders, banks and supervisors. Depending on what is happening and the level of concern, you will be meeting some groups every month, some more often and some less. All these stakeholders are extremely important for your business. Ask for their observations, feedback and advice before starting the programme and after each phase. Tell them your plans, keep them informed about progress and deliver at all times. This is the way you build solid partnerships and trust with your key stakeholders.

The two-week preparation phase

During the first two weeks before starting the programme:

1. Run my (digital) **indicative scorecard** available on: https://answerinside.eu/Book-Giveaways which will give you insights into the condition of your business and the level of complexity and urgency of the turnaround.

2. Based on discussions with your shareholders, you then need to **define the turnaround objectives**. In collaboration with HR, you should **identify the**

talent of the company using the 1 to 5 ratings as discussed in Chapter 9.

3. You will then need to **perform an in-depth diagnosis** of the business as discussed in Chapter 6 and work with finance and the management team to **get a distributed P&L and the KPIs** as discussed in Chapter 5.

4. Next, work on the **alignment with your management team** once you have the input from the previous three steps. You will usually need a two-day intensive retreat for this.

5. With the management team, apply the model presented in this chapter and tailor it to your organisation to get a **predictable process** for the Fix, Reset and Accelerate experience for your business.

6. You should then organise a **town hall meeting** to inform your entire organisation about the state of the company and the Fix, Reset and Accelerate programme. The goal of this first town hall is to have an **organisational dialogue and increase involvement**.

7. The **Turnaround DNA Programme** is then launched to start training the hero army.

8. The **Fix, Reset and Accelerate Programme** is kicked off. The Fix phase then starts.

Fix phase – months 1 to 6

In this phase the focus will be on:

1. Getting a correct monthly distributed P&L with YTD and actuals of the month, compared to budget.

2. Getting the management team members to start reporting on their KPIs.

3. Planning for the required business and profitability improvements (listed in Chapter 5) and for the issues that have come out of the business diagnosis you performed in the first two weeks.

4. Executing the business and profitability improvement initiatives. In this phase and in this step in particular, you will also be making the required interventions in your management team, as discussed in Chapter 7.

5. Improving and finalising the company-wide monitoring.

6. Aligning management and taking decisions in a weekly management team meeting.

7. Sending a weekly update to the whole organisation based on your management team meeting.

8. Holding a monthly short (preferably one-minute) engagement survey to check how employees are doing during the change in progress.

9. Holding a town hall meeting after the monthly reporting, to discuss and interact about the financials and KPIs and the progress in company and profitability improvement.

Reset phase – months 5 to 7

In month five you will start seeing your performance improve and stabilise and start seeing developments in your business in terms of engagement and morale. You then start the Reset phase to begin thinking about the future strategy, business and earning model of the business.

In this phase you will:

1. Be working with a monthly distributed P&L, with YTD and actuals of the month, compared to budget.

2. Be working with weekly KPI reporting from the management team members.

3. Build planning for the Reset phase.

4. Start working on redefining the strategy, business and earning model as discussed in Chapter 8.

5. With the training of your hero army ready, allocate them to strategic initiatives that will come out of this phase.

6. Translate your strategy into breakthrough strategic objectives, build transformation plans together with functional area owners and their project managers (from the hero army), assign the project management office role and set up the portfolio reporting, as discussed in Chapter 8.

7. Have a weekly management team meeting to align and take decisions.

8. Send a weekly update to the organisation based on your management team meeting.

9. Hold a monthly short (preferably one-minute) engagement survey to check how employees are doing and hold a monthly town hall meeting (after the monthly reporting) to discuss the financials and KPIs, the company's progress and profitability improvement and, at the end of this phase, the future strategy for the business and plan for its transformation.

Accelerate phase – months 7 to 12

In month seven your transformation plan for implementation of your new strategy will be ready, together with the portfolio monitoring and reporting. The management team will be accelerating the realisation of the breakthrough strategic objectives, supported by their trained team members in the hero army.

In this phase you will:

1. Be working with a monthly distributed P&L, with YTD and actuals of the month, compared to budget. You will probably need to update the distributed P&L based on changes the transformation is generating.

2. Be working with weekly KPI reporting from the management team members. As above, you will need to regularly update the KPIs.

3. Build a plan for the Accelerate phase.

4. Be implementing the defined strategic initiatives.

5. Have a weekly management team meeting to align and take decisions for the going concern and for the project portfolio and strategic projects.

6. Send a weekly update to the organisation based on your management team meeting.

7. Hold a monthly short employee engagement survey as above.

8. Hold a monthly town hall meeting as above.

Summary

This simple step-by-step structure for the Fix, Reset and Accelerate programme will help you manage the involvement of your stakeholders, keep monitoring the profitability and performance of the business, ensure timely decision-making with your management team, manage the big changes that need to happen, manage the flow of communication towards your organisation and keep on the top of the turnaround phases, their deliverables and how employees are feeling during the process.

I hope you now have a strong understanding of the Fix, Reset and Accelerate programme and a clear overview of what you need to do.

Key Takeaways

What you have learned in this book should help you understand what is happening in the world, how it will impact your business and what you need to do to Fix, Reset and Accelerate and get your company to thrive within twelve months.

Adapting to the changing world

The UN will be pushing the Sustainable Development Goals, the WHO will be pursuing a global vaccination solution for the COVID-19 pandemic and the WEF will push the Great Reset of the world, driven by the Fourth Industrial Revolution. These movements will shape the coming ten years. You must either step in or your business will become obsolete.

Remember that you always have control. We are all responsible for directing the evolution by how we show up as citizen, consumer or investor. You can turn the Fourth Industrial Revolution, Great Reset and Sustainable Development Goals into a force for good. This requires that you take part in shaping a future of purpose-led, inclusive, sustainable and trustworthy leadership that enhances humanity (instead of robotising it and enslaving it). A future that balances economic profit and societal value for everyone and promotes wellbeing of mankind and preservation of the planet.

For that you need to upskill and reskill your people to be able to face this evolution, align your strategy, business and earning model, align your capital allocation with drivers for long-term value creation, and strengthen your business's preparedness and resilience to crisis and environmental shocks.

If you are leading a medium enterprise you need to get involved in policy developments to ensure you are offered solutions that will help you solve real-life problems. Keep an eye on grants for SMEs – they will be coming. The medium enterprise is key to rebuilding economies and will get support through local governments.

Facing all-pervasive change and crisis

What happens around you between 2020 and 2030 has the potential to drag your business into a crisis. If the business reaches crisis point, you will need to work on a collective perception shift in your business and deploy your leadership to get your people out of this state. A Level 5 (servant) leadership, training and development of your management and employees, and an open dialogue are the solution for pulling the company out of the downward spiral. Take care of your own and your team's (mental) health during this stressful process.

Developing resilience and grit

Leading a business through a crisis and all-pervasive change will require resilience, as discussed in Chapter 3. Resilience will keep you performing at the top of your game and building and developing the right teams and organisation to accompany you on your journey.

Resilient leaders are mission-driven, whole human beings – balanced, centred, adaptable and caring. Becoming resilient requires knowing who you really are, finding your why, dealing with stress, learning to deal with difficult emotions, eliminating old limiting beliefs and developing the resilience principles and daily habits that will keep you in a positive flow.

Fixing, resetting and accelerating your business

When the business is in poor health, preferably before it becomes a bleeder, speed up the diagnosis of the business; don't start cutting costs. Look at the business holistically.

With the amount of change coming your way, you need to build your own hero army to face the change. Hiring consultants with zero experience in running businesses to fix your business is an unwise and unsustainable option. Lead the Fix, Reset and Accelerate Programme, as described in this book, together with your management team and deploy your trained hero army to speed up the turnaround. Get yourself and your team executive coaching. That is a better alternative.

If you have read this far, you are serious about changing the destiny of your business. Arriving here means you are ready to make that happen by turning around your business. Don't wait too long. Start today.

In the next section you will find resources that can support you on your journey.

Go and change your business. Put your why into practice and change the world!

What's Next?

Here are some additional resources to help you Fix, Reset and Accelerate your business in twelve months.

Indicative Business Health and Growth Diagnosis

Run the (digital) indicative diagnosis available at https://answerinside.eu/Book-Giveaways. This diagnosis is based on the diagnosis model presented in this book. In no more than ten minutes, you will gain insights into (1) the health of your business, and (2) what you need to turnaround to get it to grow and thrive fast. You will receive, directly upon completion, a free report with your scores and guidance sent to your email box.

Grow your business – Fix, Reset and Accelerate Mentoring Programmes

We crafted business mentoring programmes to facilitate business leaders and their teams who need support running their own turnaround management programme, based on the model discussed in this book. With a team of seasoned business coaches we offer the support needed to make the turnaround a success.

Turnaround DNA Programme

To support businesses in building their hero army (the top 15% talent of their company) in six months, we offer a Turnaround DNA Programme, combining online learning and live classes. This academy focuses on providing the skills needed to run all aspects of a Turnaround programme.

To find out more, visit www.answerinside.eu

Acknowledgements

Writing a book was harder than I thought. Would the ideas come on demand? Would I reach the flow necessary to deliver on time? Then you are consumed by the flow and your mind and you forget working out, eating and you lose all sense of time. It was a fascinating and consuming process, but absolutely a rewarding one. It's awesome to see how close ones, friends and my editor supported me through this process, from those who checked on me, sent me messages, and were there to brainstorm with, to those who brought food or flowers to cheer me up, proofreaders who took a walk with me to reflect or who did an amazing job reviewing every bit of the book, even the graphs. I was moved and humbled. This process opened my eyes to the goodness in people and how many great people we have in our life that are left unnoticed.

To the amazing people who came into my life, I see you, appreciate you and I am ever grateful that we were supposed to walk together for a part of our journeys in this lifetime.

To my family, those closest to my heart and the source of my daily awe and inspiration: my daughter, Sarah; my mom; my inspiring aunt and friend, Khadouj; my brother and our small heart walking on earth, Caeser. I am grateful you exist.

To my friends and my team: my forever best friend, Iris Mollet; my sister, Sharonna; my super-supportive and kind accountability partner, Petran Zuiderwijk; and my RTT buddy, Nicole Jongerius. I am grateful for our friendship.

To my amazing team and friends: Rishita Jones, Dunia Reverter, Varsham Bajnath, Rubianca Han Simmels-gaard, Joan Tjon En Fa. And to the special people who came into my life as colleagues or business partners and stayed as dear friends: Margie Zaaijer, Karima Nasr, Henk Folkers, Souad Asafiati, Buddy Willard and Eric Euwes. Thanks for being there.

To my proofreaders, a very special thank you for taking the time during your Christmas and New Year break to review my book: Hans den Hartog, thanks for the super-thorough review of my book; and Stefan Peij, for reflecting on my book and for your wise observations and feedback. A big thank you also to the people I reflected with to check my view on what is happening in the world.

To my teachers: Daniel Priestley, thank you for the amazing Accelerator programme and the constant push to 'GSD', and the great tribe I came to meet at his programme, in particular Nick, Fiona, James, Sally, Jason and Sophie.

Thanks to Marisa Peer for the inspiring Rapid Transformational Therapy programme and for impacting my view on Turnaround management and executive coaching.

To the Rethink Press team: I'm forever grateful to Roger Waltham, Geraldine Bernane, Kate Latham, Anke Ueberberg and Joe Gregory for their editorial help, keen insight, and creative support and guidance to turn this book from a dream to a reality.

The Author

Madiha Mouchtak is the Founder and Managing Director of Answer Inside, which specialises in executive coaching across Europe for leaders during times of all-pervasive change and crisis. Answer Inside helps leaders Fix, Reset and Accelerate their businesses.

A Turnaround executive, strategy and business consultant, and Rapid Transformational Therapist, Madiha has spent over twenty years working with business transformation and the rescue of failing companies, turning around businesses from loss to double-digit profit and growth. She is passionate about transformation and developing executive talent, and has extensive experience in successfully managing large-scale Turnaround programmes for strategy development and implementation, restructuring and margin improvement, and the integration of acquisitions.

Madiha has operated across a range of industries and managed companies with up to €3.5bn of assets and 5,000 employees. With an International Executive MBA in General Management, Madiha is also a Lean Six Sigma Black Belt, a member of the Turnaround Management Association (UK), a certified Rapid Transformational Practitioner and Therapist with the Marisa Peer Institute, an advisory board member of the (International) Artificial Intelligence Forum, and was named in the Women Boardroom Empowerment list in the Netherlands in 2016.

She is a super-optimist, a believer in human potential and in doing good. Her motto in life is: 'Because nothing is certain, everything is possible.'

Keep in touch with Madiha via:

in www.linkedin.com/in/madiha-mouchtak

▶ Answer Inside – Madiha Mouchtak

Printed in Great Britain
by Amazon